Residential and Commercial Service Charges

A Surveyor's Handbook

D1329336

ore

Acknowledgment

The publishers would like to thank Julian Potts of Landmark PT Ltd for his assistance and advice on the sections of this book relating to VAT.

Published by the Royal Institution of Chartered Surveyors (RICS)

Surveyor Court

Westwood Business Park

Coventry CV4 8JE

UK

www.ricsbooks.com

ISBN 978 1 84219 339 6

Typeset in Great Britain by Columns Design Ltd, Reading, Berks.

Printed in Great Britain by Latimer Trend and Company.

FSC

Mixed Sources

Product group from well-managed
forests and other controlled sources

Cert no. SGS-COC-2482
www.fsc.org
© 1996 Forest Stewardship Council

Contents

Foreword

There is a fundamental conflict at the heart of any service charge regime: the landlord is spending the tenant's money. The tenant's ability to verify that the work for which he is being charged was necessary, or was truly repair and not improvement, or to control what work was done and how, is extremely limited. As Lord Wilberforce observed as long ago as 1982 in the famous case of O'May [1983] 2 AC 726:

> 'If work can be ordered and effected by persons other than those who have to bear the cost, risks of extravagance and misdirection of effort may be created. The same separation of responsibility necessitates a system of charging by certificate and of preventing challenges, except in rare cases …'

Further potential for conflict arises from the different interests of the parties, one indefinite and the other limited in time.

Disputes about service charges are notoriously difficult to resolve. They can be very time consuming and expensive and result in great bitterness between landlord and tenant and, when funds are withheld, prejudice the running and maintenance of the building in question to everybody's detriment.

A great responsibility is thus placed on the managing agents charged with operating a service charge regime and upon those appointed to certify the expenditure. I tried to articulate this (at a much more modest judicial level than that of Lord Wilberforce) in my judgment in *Princes House v Distinctive Clubs* where I said:

> 'Tenants who agree to service charge clauses under which they contract to pay against a surveyor's estimate or an accountant's certificate rely upon the professional people involved performing their roles with professional scrupulousness, diligence, integrity and independence and not in a partisan spirit, supposing their only task to be to

recover as much money as they can for the landlord. Experience teaches that such reliance can be misplaced.'

This book will therefore prove most welcome in guiding surveyors through the separate labyrinths of commercial and residential service charge regimes, the nightmare of mixed-use developments, and in providing practical guidance on how to smooth the path, avoid the pitfalls and keep everybody happy all of the time. Good luck.

Jonathan Gaunt QC, Falcon Chambers

Preface

In writing this book we have set out to provide a basic summary of good practice in many areas in which you are likely to become involved if you manage service charges, and some guidance of how to anticipate and be prepared for what might otherwise be costly oversights.

As chartered surveyors we each specialise in what at first sight may seem very similar areas – namely residential and commercial service charges. In fact the way the law and our regulations treat them both ensure that an excellent knowledge of the one does not imply a competence to handle the other.

Many aspects of both fields are similar, but you should be warned to tread carefully when venturing from one to the other. If we were to take an every day comparison perhaps the difference between driving a powerful motor cycle and a large lorry is, to an extent, appropriate.

More recently there has been a huge increase in mixed-use developments but while the concept is not new, what is different about mixed-use developments today is the increase in the introduction of residential units into commercial buildings driven not by organic growth but by government policymaking.

All properties are unique. This inherent uniqueness in itself raises a number of issues but the mixture of commercial and residential uses, in management terms, presents particular challenges and will often require both residential and commercial service charge management skills and expertise.

As with driving, an anticipation of what may be around the corner is paramount. If we can guide you away from some of the possible pitfalls and give examples of best practice for you to follow then we will have succeeded in our aim.

Peter Forrester and Christopher Gibb

Legislation

The following Acts and Statutory Instruments are referred to in this publication. Where an Act or Statutory Instrument is mentioned frequently, it is referred to by the abbreviation in brackets that follows.

Commonhold and Leasehold Reform Act 2002 (CLRA 2002)

Companies Act 2006

Finance Act 1989

Housing Act 2004

Housing Act 1996

Landlord and Tenant Act 1985 (LTA 1985)

Landlord and Tenant Act 1987 (LTA 1987)

Leasehold Reform, Housing and Urban Development Act 1993

Limitations Acts

Local Government Act 2000

Local Government Planning and Land Act 1980

Shops Act 1950

Sunday Trading Act 1994

Administration Charges (Summary of Rights and Obligations) (England) Regulations 2007 SI 2007/1258

Control of Asbestos at Work Regulations 2002 SI 2002/2675

Construction (Design and Management) Regulations 2007 SI 2007/320

Landlord and Tenant (Notice of Rent) (England) Regulations 2004 SI 2004/3096

Service Charges (Consultation Requirements) (England) Regulations SI 2003/1987

Service Charges (Summary of Rights and Obligations, and Transitional Provision) (England) Regulations 2007 SI 2007/1257

RICS Code of Practice, *Service Charges in Commercial Property*

RICS practice statement, *Surveyors Acting as Expert Witnesses*

UK legislation passed after 1988 is published in its original form by the Office of Public Sector Information on www.opsi.gov.uk and UK legislation prior to 1988 may be purchased through the Stationary Office Limited on www.tso.co.uk.

An online database of revised UK primary legislation can be found at www.statutelaw.gov.uk, the Statute Law Database. The database is the official revised version of the statute book (primary legislation) for the UK in electronic form and contains primary legislation that was in force at 1 February 1991 and primary and secondary legislation that has been produced since that date.

1

Basic principles

A service charge is the mechanism by which a landlord, or in the case of some residential property the management company, recovers from tenants expenditure in relation to the repair and maintenance of the building, plant and machinery and the provision of services.

The fundamental distinction between residential and commercial service charges has been the introduction of statutory regulation in the residential sector, which provides protection for tenants against abuse. The *Landlord and Tenant Acts* of 1985 and 1987, subsequently amended by legislation such as the *Housing Act* 1996 and the *Commonhold and Leasehold Reform Act* 2002 (CLRA 2002), impose statutory constraints in respect of service charges for residential properties.

The commercial sector has no such statutory regulation or control.

For residential premises, section 18 of the *Landlord and Tenant Act* 1985 (LTA 1985) provides a statutory definition of a service charge as:

> 'An amount payable by a tenant of a dwelling as part of or in addition to the rent (a) which is payable directly or indirectly for services, repairs, maintenance, or insurance or the landlord's cost of management and (b) the whole or part of which varies or may vary according to the relevant costs'.

CLRA 2002 has amended this definition as amounts payable by the tenant for 'services, repairs, maintenance, improvements, or insurance or the landlord's cost of management'.

The extent to which the landlord will be obliged to provide and carry out works and services will, in respect of both commercial and residential leases, depend upon the strict interpretation of the wording of the lease.

For commercial property, where no statutory definition of service charges exists, it is generally accepted that the intention of the service charge is to put a tenant of a lease granted on internal repairing terms in a similar position to a tenant of a lease granted on full repairing and insuring (FRI) terms, otherwise known as an 'effectively' full repairing and insuring lease.

Notwithstanding the constraints imposed by statute, one of the major differences between residential and commercial services charges is the treatment of the cost of carrying out improvements. The statutory definition for residential service charges now includes provision for the cost of improvements to be recovered. This reflects the often long-term nature of most residential tenancies and the fact that the rent payable is usually fixed for the length of the term (separate rules apply for short-term lettings). However leases of commercial premises tend to be granted for relatively shorter periods with rents being subject to periodic review – usually every five years – to the open market rental value. The cost of carrying out improvements to common parts is usually seen as one which falls to the landlord.

There is also a fundamental difference in respect of the ownership of the service charge monies. Under section 42 of the *Landlord and Tenant Act* 1987 (LTA 1987) service charge contributions in respect of dwellings are to be held on trust. The service charges monies do not belong to the landlord.

However there are no such implications for the commercial sector and tenants' on-account service charge payments (usually reserved in the lease as rent) belong effectively to the landlord.

2

Reference documentation

This chapter considers the available guidance around service charges. RICS has produced a voluntary code for services charges in the commercial sector, but the RICS residential codes have statutory endorsement. This chapter looks at:

- *RICS Code of Practice: Service charges in commercial property*
- *Shopping centre marketing and promotions: Guide to good practice*
- *RICS Service charges residential management code*

2.1 RICS Code of Practice: Service charges in commercial property

Unlike residential service charges, which are the subject of statutory legislation aimed at providing protection for tenants from abuse, there is no statutory regulation or control affecting service charges in the commercial sector. Therefore, service charges for commercial property are governed principally by the law of contract and the intentions of the parties when entering into the lease arrangement

Service charges are a major source of conflict in the landlord and tenant relationship and successive governments have suggested introducing legislation similar to that which already exists for residential property into the commercial sector.

In response to this and in an effort to introduce self-regulation within the industry in 1995 various industry groups produced a voluntary *Guide to Good Practice*. On 26 June 2006 RICS, supported by various leading property industry bodies, launched the Code of Practice for*Service Charges in*

Commercial Property, which came into effect for service charges commencing on 1 April 2007. The Code supersedes the Guide and has greater prominence by virtue of its status as official RICS material.

The new Code, based on the second edition of the earlier *Guide to Good Practice* provides 'best practice' advice to practitioners and the key objectives of the Code are:

- to remove service charges as an area of conflict;
- to deliver a budgetable and forecastable part of occupiers' overheads;
- to ensure service charges that are 'not for profit, not for loss' and are cash neutral to the owners income stream; and
- to encourage transparency and communication in relation to the provision of services, their quality and cost.

The Code sets out best practice and is supported by a technical section with additional notes on specific topics and appendices which illustrate how best practice should be employed. The Code itself covers:

- management;
- communication;
- transparency;
- service standards and provision;
- administration; and
- additional shopping centre services.

The Code recognises that the best practice which is suggested for adoption is not intended to override existing leases. However, managers are expected to emulate the code and match the delivery as closely as possible despite any lease constraints that might exist.

Whilst practitioners are not required to follow the advice and recommendations contained in the Code the courts are likely to take account of the contents in reaching a decision in the event of a service charge dispute or when an allegation of professional negligence is made, because of the Code's status as an RICS guidance note.

As a result of the changes introduced under the *Civil Procedure Rules* (Woolfe Reforms), RICS intends the Code to provide access to alternative dispute resolution (ADR) for parties involved in disputes about service charges matters.

The Code is applicable in England and Wales and has been adopted with minor revisions by RICS in Scotland.

2.2 Shopping centre marketing and promotions: Guide to good practice

In May 2004 a *Good Practice Guide for Shopping Centre Marketing and Promotions* was produced by the Property Managers Association (PMA) in consultation with and supported by various industry organisations, which estimated that the UK Industry's annual spend in shopping centre marketing exceeded £80m per annum.

The *Good Practice Guide for Shopping Centre Marketing and Promotions* provides guidance in relation to the planning, formulation, consultation and success measurement of marketing and promotional planning.

The apportionment and recovery of expenditure in respect of marketing and promotions relating principally to shopping centres, as well as retail and leisure parks is a matter that gives rise to considerable debate and dispute.

Marketing and promotions are reviewed in greater detail in chapter 20.

2.3 RICS Service Charges Residential Management Code

The RICS *Service Charges Residential Management Code* has been drawn up to give advice and to provide a code of good practice in connection with the management of residential properties to which a variable service charge applies.

The Code has been approved by the Secretary of State through section 87 of the *Leasehold Reform, Housing and Urban Development Act* 1993. Separate codes have also been approved for 'rent only' residential management and for retirement housing.

Section 87 (7) provides that a failure to comply with a provision of a code will not in itself render a person liable to any proceedings BUT that a code shall be admissible in evidence to a court or tribunal. Furthermore any provision in a code which appears relevant to a court or tribunal shall be taken into account in determining a question to which it is relevant.

This can therefore be interpreted as meaning that if you follow the code you will be entitled to rely on it in any subsequent proceedings and that if you ignore it you will have to provide good reason for so doing.

A tremendous amount of consideration and effort has gone into revisions to the code over the last few years and it is designed to highlight good practice, reflecting the RICS public interest responsibilities contained in its Royal Charter. It deals with the practicalities of management and the rights and responsibilities of all those involved.

The Code is aimed at service charge management, but does not set out in detail every element of management practice. It provides a framework from which to work and indications of the appropriate statutory authority. The original Code published in 1997 consisted of the 'Rent Only' elements which formed the original Rent Only Code with further sections added to deal with service charges. Since then the Rent Only Code has been revised and approved (both for England and now Wales). The Service Charge Code revision was held off in order to incorporate the changes taking place in legislation. The revised code is specifically aimed at service charge management.

It is intended that the code be made available both to lessees and landlords, and as such it should go a long way towards explaining to both why it is necessary to undertake work in the appropriate way. Either side may not appreciate why many things need to be done and can be suspicious of each other. The code should provide assurance and often an explanation of why things are done. It also confirms things that should and should not be done.

The Code covers the following:

- appointment and charges of a managing agent;
- manager's charges where no managing agent is employed;
- managers duties and conduct;
- accounting for other people's money;
- leaseholder's right to manage;
- service charges;
- services;
- budgeting and estimating;

- reserve funds;
- accounting for service charges;
- audit or certification of service charge accounts;
- contractors;
- repairs;
- development works;
- insurance;
- information;
- residents associations;
- consultation;
- disputes between lessees;
- complaints about and disputes with managing agents by leaseholders; and
- arrears.

This is just a basic list and there are a number of additional parts covered in varying degrees of detail – the emphasis being on providing guidance for good practice where the law may be vague.

It must be remembered that the Code is aimed at putting down a basic framework for good practice which can be understood by the 'end user' without becoming overly complicated. Explaining the detailed technicalities is left for the authors to cover in this book!

The Code is intended to apply to England and Wales. Parliament in its wisdom has devolved the right to make secondary legislation in Wales to the Welsh Assembly. Under these circumstances it is hardly surprising that the Assembly exercises its right. One of the results of this is that the Rent Only revised code was adopted in England some considerable time before it was adopted in Wales.

It may just be worthwhile checking exactly which version of this or any other code or commencement order applies if you are dealing with property in both England and Wales.

3

Getting started

It is extremely important to appreciate that the rules regarding residential service charge management differ substantially from those which apply to the commercial sector. Generally the commercial sector is governed by the terms of leases while the residential sector has many statutory provisions which override the lease terms.

This chapter covers:

- Types of client
- The leases
- Available records and questions to ask about them

It is imperative that the property manager is aware of the legal rules which override lease terms, as a failure to appreciate them may be extremely costly.

The rules are dealt with later but to start with it is important to appreciate who is providing the instructions.

3.1 Types of client

Freeholder

This is the basic situation where the freehold owner has let a property and instructs you to manage it. The freeholder may be a company and may be owned by some of the lessees.

Head leaseholder

Here the freeholder has let a property on a lease which has been subsequently sublet and you act on behalf of the lessee in managing the subtenants. In practice there may be several superior leases between your client and the freeholder.

Lessee owned management company – set up under lease

It is increasingly common to see developers set up a management company under the terms of the leases on an estate for both residential and commercial leases. These can take several forms, but for residential properties common memoranda and articles of association were intended to be set up under the CLRA 2002 (at publication this section has not yet been brought into force).

Currently companies are either limited by guarantee or have allotted share capital. Generally each leaseholder is a member of the company which is responsible for the management of the service charge either entirely or subject to some exceptions (the most common being insurance).

When dealing with this type of company it is worth noting that your client may well wish you to manage its company affairs as well as the service charge. This may involve keeping and maintaining the company statutory books and share register. In addition you may be requested to act as company secretary. Before doing this you should consider any statutory liabilities that this might involve – accountants will often suggest that the company secretary has little or no liability and while this was historically usually true, new liabilities for things such as health and safety have changed things somewhat.

You may also be required to call meetings and serve statutory notices thereof. You should be aware of the time required to manage a company and that your client may be a board of directors.

These companies often have difficulties recruiting directors and as a result risk being struck off.

When dealing with residential properties the service charges are held on trust under section 42 of the LTA 1987. The service charges are not assets of the company. The company acts as trustee.

Lessee owned management company – set up under right to manage

CLRA 2002 has set up a right to manage for residential lessees. A right to manage company must first be set up in the statutory form. There are prescribed memoranda and articles of association and the company must be limited by guarantee. This means that there is no share capital but there is a list of members.

Once the company is set up all lessees must have notice served upon them again in a prescribed form inviting them to join. If lessees of 50 per cent of the units take part a notice may be served on the landlord exercising the right which takes effect in three months. The procedure must be followed correctly to exercise the right and it is open to challenge at the Leasehold Valuation Tribunal.

Before exercising this right, all the rules should be studied in detail to ensure that they are complied with.

The right to manage company is not compelled to continue with existing contracts nor does it have to use landlord nominated contractors or insurers. Exactly what repercussions there may be of rescinding certain contracts remains to be seen but the company will be in a strong position to renegotiate those which may seem over priced.

Again when dealing with this type of company it is worth noting that your client may well wish you to manage its company affairs as well as the service charge. This may involve keeping and maintaining the company statutory books and share register. In addition you may be requested to act as company secretary. Before doing this you should consider any statutory liabilities that this might involve – accountants will often suggest that the company secretary has little or no liability and while this was historically usually true, new liabilities for things such as health and safety have changed things somewhat.

You may also be required to call meetings and serve statutory notices thereof. You should be aware of the time required to manage a company and that your client may be a board of directors.

These companies often have difficulties recruiting directors and as a result risk being struck off.

When dealing with residential properties the service charges are held on trust under section 42 of the LTA 1987. The service charges are not assets of the company and the company acts as trustee.

Freeholder managed

Many large institutional owners of property prefer to manage their commercial property portfolios directly in order to reduce the costs of management and to maintain greater control over their assets. Freeholders often manage their own residential property, sometimes as a business and sometimes because they live in part of it (or did at some time in the past).

Whether or not fees can be charged for management in these circumstances will depend upon the terms of the lease. Chartered surveyors will often be called upon for advice when disputes arise or where the freeholder is unsure of the position.

With small house conversions as an example it may not be economic to undertake professional management on a day-to-day basis. In these circumstances there is a risk that small freeholders will incur costs which they cannot recover. A compromise is sometimes reached whereby major works are dealt with by a professional firm in which case this can include service of section 20 major works notices.

Intermediate landlords and recovering costs from subtenants

Particularly in the case of residential properties this can create a real problem, because in order to recover costs section 20 notices must be served on those who have to pay the bill. If you manage an intermediate interest you will need to take steps to ensure that your client's tenants receive the appropriate notices. This may well involve a need to co-operate with the superior landlord and cover reasonable costs.

A recent Court of Appeal decision may help to clarify the above position, but has further complicated matters in respect of mixed-use properties. *Oakfern Properties Ltd v Ruddy* [2006] EWCA Civ 1389 upheld an earlier County Court decision of *Heron Maple House v Central Estates Ltd* [2002] 1 EGLR 35,

[2002] 13 EG 102 which determined that a landlord of a mixed-use building that contains some residential areas, will more than likely need to follow the section 20 procedures if it intends to recover through the service charge costs for works exceeding the prescribed limits set down by statute.

In *Oakfern* it was held that a maintenance charge payable by the head-lessee was a service charge within the meaning of section 18(1) of the LTA 1985 and that the Leasehold Valuation Tribunal therefore had jurisdiction to hear an application by a subtenant to challenge the reasonableness of the service charge payable by the head lessee to the freeholder.

A 'tenant of a dwelling' within the meaning of section 38 of the LTA 1985 was not excluded from the protection afforded to residential tenants merely because, whilst he was the tenant of a dwelling which extended only to part of a building, he was also the tenant of other parts of the building. The 1985 Act speaks of the 'tenant of a dwelling' not the 'tenant of a dwelling and nothing else'.

The corollary of the decision in this case means that a landlord of a mixed-use building that contains some residential areas must follow the section 20 procedures if it intends to recover through the service charge costs for works exceeding the prescribed limits set down by statute, even though the ultimate payer of the service charge is a sub-tenant. Other statutory procedures will also need to be followed to ensure that non-recovery does not result due to an infringement of the legislation designed to protect residential occupants.

Where the intermediate lease contains both residential and commercial premises the commercial service charge would in effect no longer be governed solely by the law of contract but would also benefit from the statutory regulation usually only afforded to residential tenants.

There may be some situations where a direct covenant by the owner of one block to the owner of an adjoining property leaves the owner of the first block liable for expenses as freeholder of that block. The owner may not have the right to a section 20 notice as he or she is not a lessee yet if he or she is to recover the costs from the lessees the owner may need to serve one on them!

In such circumstances it is wise to make reasonable requests for provision of information in a spirit of co-operation.

What do you need to know about the property?

Where commercial management is concerned the main rules will be derived from the leases.

In the case of residential management the law may override many of the clauses but the starting point will still be the leases. It is only where the law steps in that things will change.

So much depends upon the lease terms and these may vary enormously.

3.2 The leases

Do they differ?

Do not assume that all leases on a development are the same. Always check to confirm the position. Unfortunately with the advent of word processors leases have become much longer which makes this task more difficult. Do not be surprised if a clause has been omitted from a few leases. Some draftsmen cut out whole sections! If you are lucky they leave the rest with the same numbering as it had before the cut, but don't expect that to be the case.

If the leases differ this may create management problems and may result in certain costs being recoverable from some tenants and not from others.

There is a general rule of law that a contract is complete and a tenant is only liable to pay a service charge or contribute towards certain costs only so far as the lease allows. The courts are reluctant to rectify drafting errors unless there is an overriding need to intervene in order to give business efficacy to the arrangement.

Are there separate schedules?

The simplest arrangements place all expenditure into a single schedule but with the advent of a desire for fairness many service charge calculations now require several schedules to which different apportionments apply.

If there are separate schedules then they must be accounted for and any surplus allowed specifically to that schedule. The calculations can be very complicated but comprehensive property management computer systems can deal with them. If you are fond of maths they can even be quite fun!

Inevitably there is more work involved when dealing with a multi-scheduled building as the budgeting has to be more precise and care has to be taken analysing invoices, some of which may have to be split before being posted to the accounting system. It will also be necessary to obtain more detailed billing from contractors.

In some cases multi-scheduling may create greater costs to those who it seeks to 'be fair to' than would have been the case under a simple system.

You must take care to ensure that all leases are checked and that your accounts system is set-up to reflect any particular references to apportionments.

Refer to chapter 8 for further details on apportionment schedules.

Is there provision for 100 per cent recovery of expenditure?

This may seem a strange question to the newcomer to this field but it is surprising how often the answer is no! The problem may only occur in one schedule or in more. It may be minor or substantial.

As above, leases may differ in their specific wording thereby creating a situation where not all costs are recoverable from all tenants. Furthermore, where fixed service charge percentages are stated in the lease, the aggregate of the percentages might add up to more or less than 100 per cent.

Where a shortfall in recovery exists the owner will usually need to make good the difference. If the property is owned by the lessees through a company then the company will need to make up the difference by a charge to its members. The liability will usually fall according to share holding which may be very different to what might have been the case had the apportionment been worked out correctly in the first place.

In the case of residential property, a shortfall may also come about as a result either of a right to enfranchise (where part of the building has been compulsorily acquired by its lessees) or by some other alteration which has benefited all the remaining lessees. In such a case the actual apportionments might be deemed to be greater than those in the leases.

For residential purposes, where the leases do not provide for 100 per cent recovery of costs incurred an application may be made to the Leasehold Valuation Tribunal for variations in some circumstances.

If the apportionments are greater than 100 per cent there are a number of ways of dealing with this but as long as the difference is not pocketed by the landlord and it remains within the appropriate schedule or reserve attached to it, it can be used to the benefit of the appropriate service charge.

In the case of commercial property if the sum of the fixed percentages stated in the leases add up to more than 100 per cent the landlord will often credit any surplus back to the service charge for the benefit of all tenants so that only 100 per cent of the actual costs incurred is recovered. However, as each lease is a separate contract there is nothing in common law to prevent the sum of the percentages adding up to more than 100 per cent. The landlord would therefore effectively make a profit from the provision of the services. While this is not illegal, it would be immoral and contrary to best practice principles.

For commercial properties, there is little that can be done to mitigate any over or under recovery of the service charge unless the occupational leases provide for the basis or method of calculating tenant apportionments to be altered or changed. Alternatively the basis or method of apportionment could be altered by mutual agreement from all parties although this is often difficult to achieve in the case of a large multi-let building particularly where there might be 'winners' and 'losers'.

What services is the landlord obliged to provide?

In simple terms the landlord is obliged to provide services specified within the lease and those further required by law (even if not included in the lease). Otherwise, in the absence of specific wording, the inclusion of an item within a service charge clause does not necessarily place an obligation on the landlord to provide that service.

The services that a landlord is obliged to provide or perform would be listed within the landlord's covenants, usually found elsewhere in the lease and separate to the service charge provisions.

Many leases contain clauses which provide for variation but many do not. If a service is clearly obsolete then it may not be possible to provide it. But beware – if it is possible to provide it and a lessee wants it the landlord may be in breach of covenant if he or she withdraws it.

For example, it can be extremely attractive to a landlord to sell the porter's flat in a small residential block particularly when there was no provision for the service charge to include a notional or deemed rent. If the leases provide for a resident porter to be included as part of the 'services' the landlord may not have the option to dispose of the flat even if only one tenant wishes the services of a resident porter to continue.

In the residential sector applications can be made to a Leasehold Valuation Tribunal to vary services in certain circumstances.

Commercial leases (and some residential) will often provide the landlord with the ability to add to, vary, amend or discontinue the provision of services either at its discretion or in accordance with the principles of good estate management. However, such clauses need to be treated with some care as often the landlord's ability to vary the services may in fact be limited and would need to be read in the context of the lease as a whole.

Health and safety legislation may require provision of certain services or a variation in the way in which they are provided.

The landlord cannot derogate from his or her grant. If the lease provides for parking in a particular area, or designates certain areas as common parts then this must be provided. The areas cannot be leased out for some other purpose or altered unless the lease provides that they can.

What services can the landlord provide at its discretion?

This depends upon the wording of the leases. If they provide for additional services at the landlord's discretion then for residential leases only reasonable additions can be made. A reasonable service will be one which a Leasehold Valuation

Tribunal (LVT) will be willing to agree is reasonable and if in doubt an application should be made to the Tribunal.

If a service is requested by all the lessees, unless there are very strong indications to the contrary then it would be reasonable to provide it. The problem comes where there is a disagreement or a slim majority. An application to the LVT might solve the problem.

Many modern commercial leases often contain provisions that obligate the landlord to provide certain services (mandatory services) while listing others that the landlord may provide at its discretion (non-mandatory services).

What costs is the tenant obliged to reimburse?

The situation for commercial lettings is that tenants are only liable to reimburse the landlord the cost of providing services so far as the lease allows.

Even under a lease that contains a detailed service charge clause, there may be landlord's expenditure that falls outside the wording of the clause and would not be recoverable. There is no presumption that service charge provisions are automatically intended to enable a landlord to recover all his or her costs for the provision of services. Furthermore, it is a common law principle that where a list of items is inserted in a lease there is an assumption that items not included are **not** recoverable.

For commercial properties, in the absence of any specific reference in the lease as to whether the cost of the supply of services should be reasonable there is an implied term that when spending the tenants' money, the landlord has an obligation not to be unreasonable.

Notwithstanding what the lease says as regards residential property, the law may well further restrict the terms of the lease. Service charges must be reasonable as determined by a Leasehold Valuation Tribunal and notice of expenditure under section 20b or a demand for payment must be given within 18 months of incurring expenditure. In addition section 20 LTA 1985 limits recovery of certain expenditure unless a notice procedure has been complied with.

CLRA 2002 places further requirements to be complied with before action can be taken for non-payment.

To an extent there is a two stage process. Firstly confirm whether monies are recoverable under the terms of the lease, and secondly whether or not the law permits recovery. Generally if the lease does not allow recovery then it cannot be made.

Do the leases differ between tenants?

It is very important to confirm the particular details of each lease as it is very common for leases to differ between tenants. It is certainly not desirable but often results from negotiations with developers. Just because one lease allows or disallows something does not mean that they all do.

Can the landlord demand service charge payments on account?

If the lease is silent then it is generally assumed that payments are to be made in arrears.

Are these to be based on a budget, previous years costs, etc.?

The lease may well set this out. If it does, the requirements as set out in the lease will need to be followed if they do not conflict with over-riding legislation.

Where the lease does provide for the service charge to be based on the landlord's estimate of the anticipated expenditure, care is needed as the requirement to issue a budget may be a condition precedent to the tenants' liability to make an on-account payment. The lease therefore needs to be read carefully and properly recorded to ensure the procedures stipulated in the lease are followed.

In the absence of a revised budget, leases will often provide for tenant's on-account payments to continue to be demanded and paid based on the previous year's estimate.

RPI indexation of accounts

These are increasingly common in commercial leases, particularly in older properties where tenants seek to cap their service charge liabilities to protect themselves from future major expenditure items.

Where a tenant's service charge liability is subject to increases in line with the Retail Price Index (RPI) the wording of the lease should be carefully considered, as often the RPI indexation would constitute a limit on the tenant's liability and not an automatic increase. Therefore, if the service charge expenditure increased below RPI, the tenant's liability would be limited to the lesser of the increase in actual costs or the increase in RPI.

Where a lease specifies a particular index, a common-sense approach is required in taking the stated index in the event that it may change and be calculated on a slightly different basis – e.g. changes to the basket of commodities, services and items included in the index. Furthermore, while a lease might stipulate a particular index, care is needed in calculating any adjustments to the service charges payable based on the correct index. Some indices might still be calculated although may not be the headline index quoted in the media, etc. – for example the Office for National Statistics publishes both the All Items Retail Price Index also known as the 'Headline rate of inflation' and the All Items Retail Price Index excluding Mortgage Interest Payments (RPIX) also known as the 'Underlying rate of inflation'.

In the unlikely or rare event that it is used in the residential sector, RPI indexation will be subject to any over-riding legislation

What are collection dates? In advance or in arrears?

Whether service charges are collectable in advance or in arrears is very important as this can have a substantial effect on cash flow. Again you need to see what the lease provides and be careful not to introduce a scheme which has an adverse effect on a tenant which is not provided for in the lease. Under certain circumstances you will have to consider this if you wish to bring in a more generous instalment plan if this incurs greater costs in any way.

Is there provision for a reserve or sinking fund?

For commercial leases the rule applies that a tenant is only liable to make contributions towards a reserve or sinking fund so far as the lease specifically allows. If a residential lease is silent it may be possible to make an application to the Leasehold Valuation Tribunal to provide for one.

What provisions are there to make management charges?

This is especially important as it may limit your ability to charge or require an agreement directly with those instructing you.

Most, but certainly not all, leases provide for the landlord to recover the costs of administering the building and the service charge.

Management fees and administration costs charged to residential dwellings will be subject to the reasonableness tests under section 19 of the LTA 1985. Section 18(3) states: 'Meaning of 'service charge' and 'relevant costs' includes overheads in the definition of 'costs'.

Unless the managing agent's fees are expressly provided for in the service charge provisions, the landlord may not be able to recover them.

If a lease provides for the cost of employing external managing agents, but does not make provision for the alternative of allowing the landlord to charge for providing his or her own internal staff, the lease would not usually allow the landlord to recover such costs.

3.3 Available records and questions to ask about them

When considering whether or not to take on an instruction it is imperative that you have as much information about the property as possible. In time the experienced manager will inevitably discover the amount of work that it may take to put what may appear at first sight to be a reasonably run property into proper order when historic problems come to light.

Have there been historic problems with collection of service charges?

You will need to look at the statements of account for the lessees to ascertain whether there are any arrears and whether or not these are of a long standing or persistent nature.

You should also ask whether or not there are any other outstanding arrears which have not been dealt with by the current managing agents. At first sight this may seem a strange question but it can happen.

You need to know the answer to this question to avoid giving incorrect answers when replying to enquiries on assignment or compiling sellers' packs.

Example

A lessee owned management company appointed a managing agent to administer the service charge three years ago. The company had previously handled its own affairs with its directors recovering service charges which they had expended from their own personal resources!

When the instruction to manage was first given the directors undertook to recover the sums due to themselves and as a result these were not shown on the service charge statements issued by the managing agents. The directors retained the day-to-day running of their company affairs and the issue of share certificates which they refused to do at assignment unless the monies due to them were cleared.

A few months after taking over the management from the original managing agents the directors explained the position to their new agents whereby they were still owed money by one lessee who has assigned twice in breach of the lease terms to provide a direct deed of covenant and procure the transfer of the share certificate. This was very 'messy' and complicated to sort out.

You may find this far fetched but it has happened!

Several lessons can be learned from the above example:

- firstly, if (and it is far from desirable) monies are due for service charges which are not included on an agents statement, the fact should be noted in such a way as to prevent information being given out which could imply that the statement represents the full debt due. This can apply equally to sums which have not yet been charged but incurred, e.g. legal fees and accounts for repairs due specifically from a tenant;

21

- secondly, that outstanding monies due may indicate the likelihood of a considerable amount of work in recovering them; and
- finally, the need to ask the correct questions before taking on management.

Broadly speaking substantial arrears will indicate likely problems while a clear account is encouraging. It would be wise to investigate the cause of the arrears before agreeing a management contract.

Have all accounts been prepared in correct form and in accordance with legislation and the leases?

When dealing with commercial property you need to check that the accounts conform to the terms of the lease. The Code of Practice for *Service Charges in Commercial Property* sets down an industry standard list of cost codes and suggests formats for the budget and certification of service charges (see appendices 2-4). While these are considered to be best practice, the lease still needs to be carefully checked to ensure that any procedure does not constitute a condition precedent.

Attention should be given to VAT requirements for commercial properties (see chapter 4 on setting up accounts systems for more information).

Special rules for residential properties

When dealing with residential property you must start with the terms of the lease and then consider how the law affects them. It is not uncommon to see accounts for residential service charges prepared by those experienced in commercial work which do not reflect the legal position.

The form of accounts for residential service charges was to have been prescribed under the CLRA 2002. Detailed consultations have taken place since the act was passed but the final form is still awaited.

You should be aware that under the original terms of section 21 LTA 1985 lessees may serve a notice requiring a 'Summary of Relevant Costs'. This must be provided within one month if the accounts are made up and six months if they are not. If the request relates to a property with four or more dwellings it must be certified by what currently amounts to a registered auditor. The lessees then have a right to inspect the relevant documents relating to the accounts.

The CLRA 2002 provides the mechanism for further amendments to Section 21 to introduce a different but tighter regime. However, practitioners should be prepared to respond to a request as a failure to comply is a **criminal offence**.

THE IMPLICATIONS OF SECTION 42 OF THE LTA 1987 ARE OFTEN NOT FULLY APPRECIATED.

This refers to residential property and provides that the service charges are held upon trust. As such whatever the lease says service charges cannot form part of any management companies assets. For the exact terms of the trust see section 42. It is very difficult to see how showing assets which are held upon a specific trust or trusts as company assets can comply with the requirements of the *Companies Act*. The fact that this has been done (in some cases) for years is no excuse.

This is not a mere debate about form but has several important implications:

1   The ownership of the company in terms of share holding may differ from the liability to the service charge.
2   Should the company fail the service charges should be protected as they are in trust.
3   Liability for shortfalls due from the company will reflect shareholding not liability to service charge.
4   If the company is made dormant it may be easier to recruit directors as they will not be signing off figures from a managing agent over which they did not exercise day to day control. A task which many would not wish to do!
5   It has been suggested that a dormant company cannot sue for service charge arrears. The action is taken by the directors as trustees.

When dealing with residential tenants you should be aware that under section 20b LTA 1985 a tenant is not liable for service charge costs if the demand for them is served more than 18 months after they were incurred unless he or she has been served with a notice within 18 months of the costs being incurred indicating that the costs had been incurred and that he or she would be required to contribute to them.

It is of course always the case that any discrepancies should be sorted out promptly but the above provides both an added incentive and potential dire penalty.

What do I need to check?

- Do the leases have more than one schedule and have the schedules been dealt with correctly?

- Have the year-end balances been correctly allocated to their schedules?

- Have the correct apportionments been used?

- Have any balancing charges been demanded?

- Are the reserve funds held correctly?

- Is there any shortfall?

- Is there any unexplained balance?

- Do the accounts conform to the requirements of the lease as amended by legislation?

If there are any problems with the above you will need to take action to resolve them.

Do the accounts balance?

With modern advanced property management software it is imperative that the initial installation of a property is undertaken correctly and that everything balances preferably to the penny. Such accuracy is not normally expected of a set of business accounts where an auditor will take a view on materiality and a relatively small difference will be judged immaterial not least because of the costs of finding the error which may well exceed it!

When it comes to service charge management for residential property, the monies involved belong to tenants who are not generally liable to pay for balancing errors or bad debts, the funds must therefore balance.

When taking over the management of a property particularly if the tenants have run it themselves it may be necessary to resolve any differences before inputting the data to your computer system.

It must be said that if you get your accounts to balance at the outset then a modern computer system (provided that it is designed to deal with service charges) will do most of the complicated calculations for you. BUT it is imperative that it remains balanced and that the year-end accounts tie in with it.

What might I look for if they are not balanced?

To an extent this is an open-ended question but it does depend on where the difference occurs. If it is within the manager's internal accounts then it may be necessary to carry out an investigation. First look for:

- balances which have been written off;
- uncollected or demanded year-end balances;
- posting of invoices to the wrong year;
- apportionments of under 100 per cent;
- accruals and prepayments;
- invoices for work relating and chargeable to specific units;
- errors in transfers between accounts (e.g. Reserve Fund and Service Charge); and
- provisions and under provisions.

If there is a difference between the manager's accounts and those of the accountants this may well be because the accountant has adopted a different convention to achieve them. Before launching into a detailed analysis of the papers it would be worth exploring this avenue. Generally these differences relate to accruals, prepayments and provisions.

Accruals

These are allowances made within any given service charge accounting period for expenditure incurred in that period but not paid, but that should feature within that specified accounting period/year. One example is the cost of the accountant's fees and any audit for the period. Others may be accounts for any other services relating to the period which are billed in arrears. Part of the costs of a major works project may be accrued for, especially if it is not being funded directly from existing reserves. You should aim to provide in full for accruals.

Prepayments

This is an adjustment made within any given service charge account for payments made in advance of services being delivered, ensuring that the expenditure features within the accounting period/year that corresponds with the period in which the services will be delivered. When an accountant is preparing trading company accounts for tax purposes he or she needs to allow for prepayments and this is also common practice for service charges in commercial property.

However, for residential property it is a very different matter. You will need to refer to the terms of the lease, but generally you should be able to charge for costs as they are incurred which means that prepayments should be avoided. There is an extremely good reason for this. The service charge needs to reflect the cash flow required to service the fund. If you need to pay the account in an accounting period then you require the funds to do so. If you include prepayments within the service charge accounts then it is likely to appear to the tenants that they have more money available than is actually the case. In effect you will need to maintain reserves to cover the prepayments and it is simpler to show the real picture of income and expenditure for the period.

Provisions

Provisions are made within the accounts for expenditure which has or will occur which is relevant to the period concerned, but for which the final cost is either not known or not agreed. These are similar to accruals but may be converted to actual expenditure before the year-end.

Example

An item of work is carried out by a contractor but because funds are not available or his or her computer has gone wrong he or she does not invoice it. A provision may be made within the management accounting system for what is due. If the account is received before the year-end then the provision becomes real expenditure. If the account comes in after then it should technically have been an accrual.

In order to make most accounting systems work to produce accurate year-end statements accruals and provisions will need to input as if they were invoices actually received. It may also be necessary to transfer these sums to a separate fund (e.g. service charge brought forward) within your management system.

It is the treatment of the above which leads to most differences between accountant's figures and those on the management system. Experience dictates that the fault can be on either side.

Accountants may not fully understand how the computer accounting system works and make alterations to the figures given to them which may or may not be correct. It is of paramount importance that if alterations are made they are verified and the computer system brought into line. If the accountant's figures are wrong then they should be corrected. If the accountant alters his or her provisions then he or she may need to make corresponding alterations on transfers to reserves.

Generally if an accountant intends to alter the figures given to him or her then you should ensure that he or she does this initially in draft form so that it can be agreed before publication of the accounts. He or she must of course produce the correct figures but equally you must let the accountant know if he or she has made a mistake.

Property managers on the other hand may choose not to prepare draft accounts which leaves the accountant to draw up his or her own. To do this he or she will need to make assumptions particularly with regard to the above. These assumptions may not tie in with the property manager's own assumptions hence the inevitable differences. For this reason it is highly desirable for the manager to produce full draft accounts from which the accountant can work. This should reduce accountancy costs and management time spent dealing with queries.

Adjustments

Most modern computer systems work on an invoice date basis to calculate the expenditure for a period which may require some alteration to ensure that expenditure is allocated to where it should be.

One frequent source of error arises where the adjustment is different to the final expenditure. If this is not corrected an error occurs as will be the case if the actual invoice is paid without reference to the provision which will then remain outstanding.

Are copies of all contracts in force available?

In order to manage a property you will need to know the full details of any contracts which are in force. This is very important where services are involved as the terms will affect the way in which you manage the property. Some contracts may be very long-term and restrictive.

You need to know if any of the following contracts are in force, the list is not exhaustive:

- **Comprehensive contracts** – These often apply to lifts or boiler plant and can cover all routine expenditure including replacement of worn parts. Where lifts are concerned new ropes may cost several thousand pounds and may be covered under such a contract. You need to know exactly what is covered to ensure that you do not pay twice!
- **Rental contracts** – These may cover anything from door entry systems to boilers and usually include maintenance but upgrading may well be a problem.
- **Energy management contracts** – These can cover all the costs of heating and hot water including fuel. You may need to ensure that the contractor is providing what he or she is supposed to and conforming to the law regarding storage and transmission of hot water. He or she may have a financial interest in maintaining heating to the minimum within his or her contract!
- **Employment contracts** – You will need to know the terms and conditions of any employees and to ensure that employment law is complied with.

Are the contracts assignable if the property is recently acquired and are they enforceable?

The status of the contracts needs to be confirmed.

With regard to residential service charges under the terms of the CLRA 2002, it is necessary to serve notices if long-term agreements are to be entered into which would involve expenditure by any leaseholder in excess of £100 in any service charge period.

There are also provisions regarding entering into agreements on estates prior to properties being sold. See section on long-term agreements.

If Right to Manage is invoked then this may lead to contracts being frustrated. You should study the terms of the contract in the light of the law to confirm the position.

What do I need to ask about any problems with collections in the past?

While the history of problems will not necessarily reflect what will happen in the future it will give you an idea of what to expect and you would be wise to plan how to deal with potential future problems.

The following questions may be asked:

- Do the arrears result from a general dissatisfaction with the management?
- Do they result from a lack of timely demands and reminders?
- Has there been a failure to identify and deal with assignments?
- Do they result from intentional non-payment until the last moment?
- Do they result from a genuine inability to meet the level of service charge?

The first three can be dealt with by good management.

Intentional non-payment can be addressed by early resort to legal action or chasing lenders although this has cost and time implications for the service charge and your management time.

A genuine inability to meet service charge costs will inevitably lead to management problems and extra work. It may be that efficiency savings can help but the need to provide reserve funds where this occurs to smooth out charges will be paramount. In residential developments Housing Benefit is available to cover service charges but is not retrospective hence the need to alert those in reduced circumstances to the possibility of help from this source.

You may consider offering monthly payment schemes but you must consider the requirements of the leases and the possibility of those who are willing to pay on time objecting to financing those who do not. In addition you need to consider cash flow and the fact that monthly payments will not provide the last twelfth of an annual collection until the last month of a year (assuming everyone pays in advance!). If you have large annual bills to pay during the year you will need reserves to meet them which will mean higher overall bills. You also need to consider the accounting costs involved with monthly payments and the time it will take to post and verify the entries.

It is worth noting that the cash flow from annual or half-yearly bills is usually much better than for monthly ones. One compromise is to send an annual bill with a concession that provided everything else is paid up by a given date half the annual charge due may be paid at a later date unless an assignment takes place in which case the account should be brought up to date.

Experience shows that this often secures prompt payment of the first half and any arrears. If it is not paid then action can be threatened to recover the full amount due. It also secures full payment of the annual bill from those who do not like outstanding accounts.

You should be aware that the offer of a discount for prompt payment is unlikely to conform with the terms of most leases although interest on late payment may well do so.

Have the accounts been prepared consistent with the leases as amended by the law?

It is very important to ensure that accounts prepared are consistent with the lease as amended by law – see also the previous section on page 20 discussing available records.

Are there any current disputes?

Before taking on any management you should find out whether or not there are any on-going disputes. If there are you should investigate their true nature and history. When dealing with residential property in particular you must appreciate that you are dealing with a person's home and in many ways tenants will be more emotive or concerned about any dispute involving it than might otherwise be the case.

There are of course many commercial disputes and the sums at stake may be substantial. You should consider the resources which will have to be invested to resolve these disputes and ensure that your clients are aware of the likely costs to them of this work.

It is also important that you appraise the situation fully and make a positive decision on whether or not you wish to be committed to following through all the necessary work required to put the estate into an orderly and well managed situation.

It is better to decline at an early stage rather than wish to give up halfway through.

4

Setting up the accounts system

The property management accounting system will form an essential part of your business and without an efficient and appropriate system you will be severely restricted in your ability to provide a cost effective service. It is essential that this field is treated as a pivotal part of your business and not just an 'add on'. This chapter includes:

- What is needed?
- Consider the future
- Provision to comply with the law and RICS Accounting rules
- Time limits and interaction with service charges
- What to look for in a system

4.1 What is needed?

While it is still possible to keep service charge accounts using written ledgers, in practical terms this cannot be cost effective on a commercial basis. Indeed, with many larger multi-let commercial properties this would be almost impossible.

It is also possible to manipulate spread sheets in order to carry out apportionments on multi-scheduled properties and produce all the necessary accounting but as the business grows a multifunctional accounting system will become increasingly necessary.

It takes a considerable amount of time to transfer records from one system to another all of which must be seen as wasted if it could have been avoided. Of course it is often cost effective to transfer from a bad system to a good one, but far more so to have picked the good one in the first place!

Buying the right system for your business

When considering the costs of your system remember that the system cost itself is only the headline capital cost. You should also bear in mind:

- **Staff training costs** – These are not only the cost of seminars and suppliers training but the real cost, in time and mistakes, of staff learning how the system works which will be considerable.
- **Input time** – This is the initial time spent inputting data which will again be considerable and vary according to the system chosen.
- **Transfer time** – If you need to transfer to a new system because you have outgrown the capabilities of your old one then this will be considerable and the more data on your old system the more costly it will be.
- **Protection against corruption by employees** – You should assess the susceptibility of the system to being corrupted by incorrect use by an employee. The more advanced systems provide different levels of access which can be set for employees according to their capabilities (e.g. view only or alter notes, etc.) up to full access to alter the entire system. This facility is extremely important as the costs of tracing and correcting rogue entries deep in the system can be considerable. Those responsible may well have made them in blissful ignorance of the damage which they were causing and will invariably be unable to explain at a later date exactly what they did. Experience suggests that this often involves:

  - continuing to press buttons once someone has become lost in the vain hope that this will 'Put things Right';

  - temporary staff and those without specialist knowledge of the system may need to be given access but prevented from altering the set-up; and

  - fraud, which is something we all hope will not occur but prevention is very important and to this end the system you choose should be able to assist you in this field.

What is available?

Format	Description	Advantages	Disadvantages
Paper ledgers	Written by hand.	Low capital cost. Can be used by the computer illiterate.	Very time consuming. Provides single source of information. Very high labour costs to maintain and audit. Increasingly obsolete. Difficulty in obtaining skilled staff to operate.
Basic electronic ledgers	Entered on spreadsheets or general accounting programmes.	Low capital cost.	Time consuming. Provides information in a basic form. Higher audit costs. Will require specific knowledge of system to operate. Will require the use of spread sheets to calculate apportionments and manual integration. If complicated apportionments and scheduling are involved a high skill level will be required to operate. Can be very open to corruption of data. Only suitable for relatively small scale operation.
Basic rent accounting packages	Computer system designed for rent collection often used by letting agents.	Lower capital cost.	These systems are designed to account for rents collected for landlords. They may not include purchase ledgers and do not include service charge accounting systems. They can be used in conjunction with spread sheets to demand service charges but apportionments will also need to be carried out on a spread sheet and manually transferred to demands on the system. If complicated apportionments and scheduling are involved a high skill level will be required to operate. The spread sheets can be very open to corruption of data. Only suitable for relatively small-scale operation. Unless you already have a Rent Accounting Package this system is unlikely to be suitable.

Custom designed integrated systems	Computer system designed for specific requirements of your business	In theory obtaining exactly what you want from a system. In the past this may have been cost effective. Some existing systems work very well for their users.	Initial cost. Ongoing development costs. Need for specific staff training. Need to keep up with rapidly changing property legislation. Need to keep pace with developments in other computing programmes.
Fully integrated property management systems	Computer system designed to cope with all aspects of property management including service charges. These systems can also have capabilities extending to full order processing, progress chasing, remote access via modem, full document storage and retrieval via scanning, diaries, agreements, standard letters, leases and virtually everything required for a paperless office.	The larger providers have teams working on development. The system should cover everything you are likely to need. Custom features for your firm can be designed at a cost. Many systems are sold by module enabling you to buy what you require and add in the future. The system has been developed so glitches should be avoided (but they do occur).	Initial cost and ongoing costs. Need for specific staff training although some of the larger systems are widely used. Need to ensure that the system you buy actually does what you require. These systems are now very sophisticated and if they are to be used to their best advantage an experienced member of staff will have to put in a lot of time ensuring that you get the best out of the system. Some of the features are ideal for large organisations but too time consuming for smaller ones. Charges are often based on user licences per computer.

Which one do I choose?

This will depend on where you wish to go – at the end of the day if you wish to grow beyond a small operation then the fully integrated management system must be the first choice. You need to make sure that whichever method you pick does all that you want it to. Nowadays there is a need to deal with increasingly complicated multi-scheduled properties which operate at several levels (e.g. estate charge paid by all, several different blocks charged in varying ways, etc.) and within each of them a number of different schedules. If you are likely to deal with this type of estate make sure that the system you choose will handle it.

At the time of writing the government is still considering introducing rules requiring each schedule to be held in a separate account when dealing with Residential Property. You are likely to need a system which can handle this and preferably produce integrated accounting statements for leaseholders.

There is a large time cost involved in initial input but this should generally be handled by your staff as your business expands. The cost of repeating this in order to upgrade to a better system will grow as your business does. You should therefore look to install a system which will be suitable for your requirements as you grow. It is bad enough learning how to work one system without having to repeat the process when you out-grow it!

How do I use my system once I have got it?

Experience suggests it would be best to start off using the accounting system correctly and move on from there. If you attempt to start the accounting in a piecemeal way, the longer you carry on the worse your problems will become.

The larger your business becomes the more difficult it will be to get your system to work properly if you have been using it incorrectly.

You should always ensure that your system balances individual properties and schedules at the year-end and that whatever the accountant or auditor produces ties in with your system. If there is a difference between the accounts and your system it should be reconciled without delay. You may have an error or the accountant may have misinterpreted your figures. In either case it is of paramount importance that the difference is cleared up as soon as possible because the longer it is left the more difficult it generally is to correct.

If you are dealing with VAT returns or service charges you must ensure that the system is set-up properly at the start. These matters are dealt with in greater detail later in this chapter.

It is often necessary to apply dates to purchase invoices which bring them into the accounting period to which the expenditure relates. In other cases it is often appropriate to make provisions which are later settled from a separate brought-forward fund attached to the property account and used to deal with accruals.

When dealing with new part-occupied developments and properties where service charge apportionments change during the year it may be necessary to carry out manual calculations rather than using the automatic system until a period of full occupation commences. It may also be necessary to carry out manual adjustments where changes occur during a year. Many systems work very well on a whole year basis but you need to know exactly what they do (and confirm that this is what you require) if apportionments change during the year.

If you are operating a medium-sized business you should consider the advantages of the added features offered, e.g. order processing, paperless office, remote access, etc. Some businesses may find they can operate without these features as they do not directly affect the accounting records, but they can be added as and when needed on a piecemeal basis.

VAT

VAT is a complex subject and the authors do not intend to cover it in depth in this book. Advice should always be obtained from accountants or tax experts as appropriate. It is however important to highlight the differences in the treatment of VAT between the commercial and residential sectors as these can have a major impact upon the recoverability and level of service charges.

The commercial sector

Supplies of land and buildings, such as freehold sales, leasing or renting, are exempt from VAT. It therefore follows that rents received by landlords that include service charges are not generally subject to VAT. NO VAT is added on to the sum demanded for rent, etc. and no input VAT is recoverable on expenditure either by the landlord or the tenant.

As tenants are accustomed to charging VAT on the goods they sell and recovering the VAT that they have had to pay to their suppliers, many did not readily understand why they were unable to recover the VAT element paid by the landlord and included in the service charge.

Following changes introduced under the *Finance Act* 1989, landlords are now able to make a once-and-for-all election to waive the exemption on commercial rents and service charges (also known as an option to tax). The effect of such an election is to make the rents and service charges liable to VAT at the standard rate.

The landlord can then recover the VAT which he or she has incurred in the provision of the services and maintenance and upkeep of the building, and will charge the tenants VAT at the standard rate on both the rent and service charge.

Where the tenant is 'a fully taxable person' and has the right to recover the VAT on his or her overheads in full, the tenant's position will not be jeopardised. This is not the case where tenants are exempt of partially exempt – the need to take advice cannot be over emphasised.

An option to tax can only be exercised by landlords who are registered for VAT. If not registered, then rents, etc. are outside the scope of VAT.

Whether a landlord has or has not exercised an option to tax, VAT is a complex topic and the extent to which VAT is recoverable by the landlord will be dependent upon the landlord's particular circumstances. The landlord's accountant will advise on VAT matters.

Change of landlord

It is important to highlight that in the event of a change of landlord the option to tax ceases. Unless the vendor applies the transfer of a going concern rule (TOGC) VAT will be added on the sale price for the property

In order to reclaim the VAT on the purchase price, the purchaser will probably opt to tax the property but the purchaser does not have to exercise the option to tax. In such circumstances, particularly where the existing managing agent is retained by the new owner, it is essential for the managing agent to alter his or her records to reflect the revised VAT treatment for the property to ensure that demands issued to tenants and payments made to suppliers are treated correctly.

The residential sector

Dwellings and residences are exempt from VAT. Therefore, all service charge demands will include any input VAT payable (i.e. the VAT charged by suppliers of goods and services to the property).

If suppliers do not charge VAT (generally because they are below the registration limit) or supplies are not liable to VAT (e.g. certain employees wages) care should be taken to ensure that these costs do not pass through a third party who needs to charge VAT, if it can reasonably be avoided, as this will not be recoverable.

Mixed-use properties

Mixed-use properties can create particular problems due to the potentially different VAT treatment of the commercial and residential elements.

If the landlord has not opted to tax both the commercial and residential elements will be 'exempt' for VAT purposes and would be treated identically. However, if an option to tax is made the commercial element would be standard rated while the residential element would remain exempt.

In these circumstances, two sets of accounts will be required, with all expenditure incurred in respect of the commercial and residential elements kept separate and treated accordingly for VAT purposes. Where expenditure is incurred which is common to both elements of the building (e.g. repairs to roofs or other common structure) expenditure needs to be apportioned between the different elements of the building and the apportioned VAT element of the invoices treated as appropriate.

VAT operating requirements

Where the landlord is administering his or her own property, then he or she is acting as principle and must account for the VAT through his or her own VAT return. Where the agent issues invoices in the name of the landlord, the agent has to account to the landlord for all the output and input VAT.

Sometimes, landlords collect rents directly, and their agents administer the service charge in which case the agent accounts to the landlord for all service charge VAT (both input and output) or the agent acts as principal for service charge VAT, and accounts through his or her own VAT return.

Recovery of input VAT on opted properties is dependent on suppliers rendering invoices in the correct name, i.e.:

- to the landlord – landlord recovers
- to the landlord c/o the agent – landlord recovers
- to the agents – agent recovers.

Incorrectly addressed invoices can affect the recoverability of VAT. Where agents are placing orders/contracts on behalf of a landlord it is therefore vital that suppliers understand to whom they are to invoice

It is also vital that the agent understands that if goods are invoiced to it at its request it is ultimately liable for their settlement.

Different systems operate in various ways. It cannot be over emphasised that accounting differences thrown up by the system should be resolved at the earliest opportunity as if they are left it will inevitably take a lot longer to correct them.

Note for residential agents taking on commercial work

If you are operating in the residential market you may not need to make VAT returns on individual clients or service charge accounts and you may operate your system successfully without any problems. If you then decide to take on work which requires full VAT accounting then you may find that your system set-up is not compatible with this work.

You may also find that miss-postings which do not matter in the 'Gross' world do in the 'net + VAT' world.

Examples:

- The system is installed with default VAT settings for each supplier. If the Gross figures are all that matters the staff will simply post and ignore what the system does with the VAT as long as net + VAT = Gross. This can lead to a miss-posting which does matter when VAT is to be reclaimed, e.g. the VAT rate is other than the default as is often the case for example with electricity 5 per cent or 17.5 per cent.

- The staff simply ignore what the system does with regard to VAT. This may create no problem with gross accounting. They will need to consider exactly what they are doing and be trained how to deal with VAT. It will be necessary to check that they are operating the system correctly and that any bad habits are eradicated promptly.

It is essential that you ensure that you fully understand how your system is dealing with VAT and that this is compatible with the way in which you need to treat it. If you are not careful you can inadvertently move funds from a service charge account to an owner or vice versa and the complexity of some systems can make it difficult to trace exactly what has happened. If VAT refunds go direct to a client corresponding contra entries must be made at the time to account for this.

You must also understand that staff who are used to dealing with non-VAT accounting and who accomplish this task extremely well may not understand exactly how VAT is treated by their system.

Some important points:

• When preparing accounts take care to ensure that you are not confused by VAT.

• The accounts will be on a net basis but your arrears list may be gross.

• Check the basis of VAT accounting set within your system on outputs (rent, service charge, etc.) Is it date of invoice or date of receipt? If the former VAT on arrears at the year-end will have been included in the VAT return, if the latter it will not. Unless of course you have prepared the return independently of the system!

The best advice that we can give is that you ensure that you know exactly what your system is doing and that you appreciate that systems can operate VAT in a very complicated way.

Service charges

As there are so many systems available it is difficult to deal with this topic. It is also clear that some systems are evolving more quickly than others. Set out below are some general pointers towards what you should be able to achieve:

• Generally you should be able to operate a multi-scheduled property through your system. You must ensure that all schedules are properly entered at the outset and that the apportionments are installed correctly. Some systems will correct to 100 per cent if the total adds up to more. Others will automatically round the last entries to achieve 100 per cent. *(Caution: While a rounding up or down of 0.00001 per cent may be appropriate knocking off a much larger figure from one unit is not. Check that the machine has not made any inappropriate alterations.)*

• You should be able to add different cost headings within schedules at any time without causing too many problems but your system may be the exception to the rule!

• Changing apportionments during a year may cause problems.

• You need to ensure that postings of invoices are made to the correct schedule.

• The system should be designed to collect in varying apportionments according to schedule and allot expenditure to each schedule. At the year-end it will make a calculation allowing credits and charging debits to each schedule, and producing individual accounts for each unit.

- Most systems are driven by the invoice date and it will therefore be necessary to ensure that the date entered on the system is appropriate for the date on which the work was carried out.
- Where invoices cover more than one schedule it will be necessary to split them down before posting.
- You must be very careful to ensure that money belonging to one schedule does not find its way into another. At the year-end each schedule will need to be balanced with credits or demands. You must not lump any balance together as a general reserve as this may amount to directly benefiting some tenants at the expense of others. In fact this may result in your being called upon to refund money from your own funds particularly if it cannot be recovered elsewhere.
- It is not good practice to roll balances forward at a year-end. If you have a multi-scheduled property it will result in inappropriate demands and varying balances which do not reflect requirements. If a reserve is required a charge to a separate reserve fund for each schedule should be made at the year-end. If the reserves are required and permitted under the lease a final transfer to reserves of the surpluses after all other charges have been made should return your accounts to a zero balance and enable you to roll forward clear into next year.
- In order to achieve zero balances it may be necessary to make provisions or accruals as charges at the year-end for items like accountancy. In some systems a Service Charge brought forward fund may need to be set-up from which these provisions may actually be settled at a later date. This fund may also be used for recharges to tenants especially where recovery may not be guaranteed. If the recoveries are indeed made at a later date then they can be transferred back into the accounting period in which they are received. This avoids the risk of a non recoverable shortfall.
- Avoid prepayment accounting if at all possible as this is not generally compatible with systems and will produce cash flow problems. It also presents an opportunity for the accountant's figures to differ from yours – the two should be the same! You should also consider this in the light of the law and leases which usually provide for costs incurred during a period to be included in it.
- You should consider changing renewal dates for contracts rather than using prepayments.

- If your system is up-to-date and working properly and you have balanced it by the time it reaches the accountant then his or her job will be much easier as should yours.

Initial set-up

Although you can add features to your system at a later date it is well worth noting that time can be saved if thought goes into exactly how you are to set-up initially. For example, many systems allow you to copy features from a previous entry so for example if you are setting up a property with 50 flat units the features of each unit and its codings can be copied from the previous unit. If you miss out a code or other piece of information common to the building you may find yourself needing to manually alter 50 individual units at a later stage! The degree of ease with which this can be accomplished varies between systems.

Codings

It may be possible to code individual units so that specific reports can be obtained. Applying a code to those accounts which merit close and regular scrutiny could produce a report which avoids time consumed wading through other information.

Example

If you have a number of tenants whose payment records merit very close scrutiny you could code these so that a specific, even daily arrears report on those tenants could be run off. This would enable credit control to save time searching through a longer report or looking into each individual account.

You should be able to set-up your system to suit your business. There is an enormous temptation to produce huge all encompassing reports and of course these have their place. If you wish to get your system to make best use of time and maximise performance the use of shorter and more relevant reports should achieve this.

You should take care to plan your codings and descriptions so that they achieve what you require.

4.2 Consider the future

Where do you want to be in five years' time?

Property management systems are not cheap but as they are often priced on user licences (one licence per computer used by the system) entry level pricing need not be horrendous. It might be convenient to have the system on every desk in the building but is it essential? On the other hand the ability to move from 3 users to 30 if you need to is far more important. Generally adding extra licences is a simple matter and remote access is increasingly becoming available.

You really do need to assess where you intend to be in the future when you consider which system you intend to use. If you work very closely with other firms then it goes without saying that what they do may also be relevant. It may also be worth considering whether you can share expertise with them.

Problems associated with the large firm

Large firms can and always did have the money to employ an accounts team and nowadays this will include computer experts whose knowledge of the system they use should be extensive. As the system develops they need to spend the necessary time to learn exactly how it works and adapt this to the way their department works. That is not to say that large firms have an easy time as sheer volumes can often become overwhelming and mergers and acquisitions can be extremely complicated.

As property management accounting is a specialist field it may prove hard to recruit and retain staff with the necessary knowledge, experience and lateral thinking required to produce optimum results.

Problems associated with the small firm

Small firms can use less technology but need to rely on the expertise of the principal more. They can use a property management system but operate less of its more advanced features – or because the principal has to operate the system himself he or she knows exactly what he or she wants it to produce and can devise his or her own ways of achieving the requirements.

This may work well but it will eat into professional time which cannot be charged elsewhere and if key members of staff are indisposed the business will be put under pressure.

As developments are made it will often be difficult to upgrade due to the amount of staff time required to implement them.

In any event the small firm is unlikely to deal with large numbers of complicated service charges unless it specialises in them.

Problems associated with medium-sized local firms

The medium-sized firm has to contend with being stuck in the middle. It is too big for the individual hands-on approach and needs to employ a small accounts department, but this is often too small to justify a full time expert in computer property accounting in addition to its accounts clerks. In this day and age it is not possible to be competitive without an efficient property management system but it is important to assess how one can be used to its maximum efficiency and which additional features will really be cost effective.

Some additional features which are essential to the large firm may not be so to the medium-sized concern. While a full and effective use of the accounting features is essential, you will need to assess the time savings from other features.

It may be appropriate to use some features from the start, but the expense of full conversion to a 'paperless system' may not be cost effective.

If you can swap notes and experience with other firms this will be invaluable.

Cost of swapping systems (benefits of planning)

It is not always possible to swap data electronically from one system to another and the cost of doing so may be substantial. If you outgrow your system and have to swap to another you may not only need to enter all the data again but your staff will need to learn to use the new system. It is almost inevitable that the costs of the exercise will substantially outweigh the amount you saved by buying a cheaper system in the first place.

If you were starting fifteen years ago the costings may be justifiable but with modern systems and wage costs you really do need to look to the future when you make your choice. We cannot know where we will be in ten years time but before you make the investment in a new property management system and the associated staff time in implementing it, it is well worth considering the question.

Examples:

If you wish to work remotely from a tax haven at some future time, then the paperless office module will be useful for remote access!

In a similar vein if you want to expand throughout the country by use of home-based staff then the paperless office will enable remote access to the data stored on the system. This can include scanned copies of all correspondence, leases, and other documentation. At one time remote access was generally only available by use of a secure ISDN line but it is now moving into the realms of mobile technology.

4.3 Provision to comply with the law and RICS accounting rules

It may come as a surprise to many readers but there are property management systems that have features on them which are directly incompatible with RICS regulations. When purchasing a system RICS members should ensure that it is capable of complying with the rules and be sure that this is the default rather than an option.

The CLRA 2002 makes provision for the holding of service charges in separate accounts and your system should be capable of operating within the new rules which are potentially very complicated if fully enacted.

If you are or have a partner or director who is an RICS member you should also be complying with the RICS rules.

For details on the new RICS Rules of Conduct please visit www.rics.org/newregulation.

When do these rules not apply?

They apply to all client money but do not apply to funds which are not client money usually where there is joint control with the client of his or her own money. Residential service charges are always client money as they come under section 42 LTA 1987. The client even if he or she is the payee holds the money upon a statutory trust.

4.4 Time limits and interaction with service charges

There are various very important time limits for dealing with service charges and while the commercial sector is generally regulated by the lease the residential market is bound by statute. These statutes include:

Section 21 LTA 1985 as amended

This provides that service charge accounts must be distributed within six months of the year-end.

Before the 2002 Act this applied when a notice was served or had been served in the past. It is intended that it should apply in any event. Failure to comply with section 21 is a criminal offence!

Section 20b LTA 1985

This limits recovery of service charge expenditure incurred more than eighteen months before a demand is made unless notice of the expenditure has been given to the tenant during that period indicating that the tenant will be required to contribute to it.

The Code of Practice for *Services Charges in Commercial Property* sets down the following time limits:

1   The owner will provide an estimate of likely service charge expenditure and appropriate explanatory commentary on it to the occupiers, together with their proportion of the costs, one month prior to the commencement of the service charge year.
2   The owner will submit certified accounts to the occupiers in a timely manner and in any event within four months of the end of the service charge year.

4.5 What to look for in a system

Subject to the points discussed above:

- service charge compatibility;
- RICS compatibility;
- extensive support and backup;
- capacity for expansion;
- tried and trusted;
- value for money; and
- capable of meeting current and future needs.

5

Standardised form of accounts

Under existing statute there is an intention that residential service charges should be presented in a standard format. This chapter focuses on accounts for residential properties providing detail of the background and model accounts.

5.1 Residential properties – the background

Section 21 LTA 1985 gave lessees the right to make a request for a summary of costs to be provided within six months if the accounts had not been drawn up. If they had they were to be provided within one month or six months from a twelve month period end whichever was the longer.

Unfortunately the section then went on at subsection (5) to indicate what the summary should state in such a way as to cause some confusion.

Firstly, certain grants had to be shown if they applied these were the exception rather than the rule.

Secondly, three further requirements were made which were intended to deal with accruals, prepayments and creditors at the year-end. These require summaries of each of the following items:

- any of the costs of which no demand for payment was received by the landlord within the period;
- any of the costs in respect of which a demand for payment was so received but no payment was made by the landlord within the period; and

- any of the costs in respect of which a demand for payment was so received and payment was made by the landlord within that period.

The summary was also to specify the aggregate of the sums received during the period of on account of service charges and the sum standing to the credit of the tenants at the end of the period.

If the summary referred to a property comprising more than four dwellings then it had to be certified by what now amounts to a registered auditor.

The rights to inspect which follow on are dealt with in chapter 25.

Problems which have arisen include:

- Failure to comply is a criminal offence
- Interpretation of rules
- What are prepayments?
- What are accruals?
- What are creditors at the year-end?
- Treatment of accruals and prepayments

Failure to comply is a criminal offence

Section 25 LTA 1985 makes a failure to comply with sections 21, 22 or 23 a criminal offence. Indeed there have been occasions where prosecutions have taken place over the precise form of the accounts.

This section has now come home to haunt the CLRA 2002 which provides for the replacement of the old section 21 with a new one designed to curtail the ability to recover any service charge unless the accounts in a prescribed form have been provided within six months of the year-end. On balance perhaps a fair sanction. What was not fully appreciated was that a failure to comply with providing the accounts in the prescribed form within the time limit would also be a criminal offence. Whereas the 1985 rule required a request to be made before section 21 kicked in, the new rule was to apply in all cases.

While it is true to say that the requirement for an accountant's certificate could be limited to buildings containing a specific number of flats. The requirement to provide accounts in the statutory form will apply in all cases if the section is enacted.

Interpretation of rules

Unfortunately the responsibility for prosecuting lies with the local authorities which could result in differing interpretations arrived at by those whose main area of work does not lie in the field of service charge management.

The RICS *Management Code* of 1997 contains three examples of service charge accounts two of which can be seen to provide information to strictly comply with an interpretation of the rules rather than indicate a clear comparison of expenditure from year to year.

In fairness, consultation which has taken place on the new prescribed form of accounts for CLRA 2002 has moved towards a format which can be easily understood containing relevant information and some uniformity. While the type and amount of information required has been revised substantially and, at the time of writing the final document had still not been published, the more pedantic interpretations of the 1985 Act were ruled out at an early stage.

What are prepayments?

This is an adjustment made within any given service charge account for payments made in advance of services being delivered, ensuring that the expenditure features within the accounting period/year that corresponds with the period in which the services will be delivered. Generally these are used where expenditure (insurance for example) covers parts of two different accounting periods.

What are accruals?

As discussed in chapter 3 these are allowances made within any given service charge accounting period for expenditure incurred in that period but not paid, but that should feature within that specified accounting period/year. Examples include: The accountants fee for the audit of the period; management fees for a period charged after it has ended; or the estimated costs of works carried out during a period which is to be billed at a later date.

What are creditors at the year-end?

This section simply refers to monies owed to suppliers which have not been paid by the end of the year. This would typically include situations where settlement terms allowed for delayed payment.

Example: If suppliers' terms all allowed settlement 30 days after the end of the month in which their goods or services were invoiced and the year-end was 31st December then assuming that you took full advantage of the terms and settled on time. Your year-end creditors would include all December invoices.

Treatment of accruals and prepayments

Although section 21 of the LTA 1985 clearly sets out to identify accruals and prepayments it attempted to explain what they were without specifically naming them and arguably totally confused what was required.

Residential service charges need to reflect expenditure and demands made during a period and any later ones that refer to that period but whereas company accounts are concerned with reflecting profit and loss and tax liability, service charges deal with recovering actual costs incurred.

It is not generally desirable to borrow money and in many cases the costs thereof cannot be recovered.

Generally as cash flow is required to pay accounts if prepayments are included in accounts cash flow problems will result. This is because the service charges are required to meet all expenditure. If you have to pay the whole premium for insurance in a year then presenting accounts which put part of the liability into the next year will give the impression that more money is available at the year-end than is actually the case as the insurance has been paid.

On the other hand it is appropriate to fully allow for and include accruals – this will enable a true picture of the cash flow available for expenditure in future periods to be produced.

Generally after initial contract payments have been covered the service charge will settle down to reflect true annual costs with a year's charges falling into each period.

Where service charges are collected other than annually and contracts are payable annually you will either need to retain reserves to settle them, time settlements towards the year-end or spread them throughout the year on a balanced basis.

5.2 Model accounts

Residential sector

Included as Appendix 1 is a sample set of residential service charge accounts. These may be superseded by a prescribed set should the Government bring one in.

Important notes:

In a case where the expenditure is extensive then if the income is placed after the expenditure rather than before it may be easier to read and tie in for the lessees as the total income and expenditure will come on the same page.

It is also important to deal with balancing charges for a previous year in such a way as not to show them as income due for the current period – the lessees need to know the actual annual cost of running the account in any given year and year-on-year balancing charges can distort this unless they are dealt with so that they do not.

Section 21 LTA 1985 as amended by CLRA 2002 provides for a prescribed form of accounts which will take precedence over this example if and when it is enacted.

It is very important that section 21 LTA 1985 certificates are issued to conform with the Act. Before issuing accounts you should consider them in the light of the wording of the statute as amended at the time to ensure that they comply.

Commercial sector

The RICS Code of Practice for *Service Charges in Commercial Property* includes a set of industry standard cost codes which have been drawn up in conjunction with OSCAR™ (Office Service Charge Analysis Report) and ITOCC (International Total Occupancy Cost Code), which is included as Appendix 2.

6

Record keeping

In the past it was necessary to keep good records in order to facilitate excellent and efficient estate management. This has not changed but nowadays a failure to keep records may well result at best with an inability to recover costs and at worst with a potential criminal conviction. This chapter discusses:

- Your role
- Basic essentials
- What you must keep
- What else you should keep
- Other records you may be called upon to maintain
- Importance of accuracy
- Special requirements for houses in multiple occupation

6.1 Your role

This will of course depend on the instructions which you have received and the extent to which you are to be involved but generally the more records which are held the easier it is to manage smoothly.

6.2 Basic essentials

The following will be required:

- names and addresses of all tenants;
- names and addresses of any guarantors to the leases
- details of demises;
- all apportionments;
- names and addresses of clients;
- names and addresses of superior landlords;

- all relevant lease details including dates, service charge periods, etc.;
- details of any formal recognition of a residents' or tenants' association;
- copies of any past accounting records;
- copies of any ongoing contracts or guarantees; and
- any CDM manuals or M and E drawings.

If you are responsible for insurance then you will need detailed records of claims, valuations, usage and other matters of relevance. You will need to comply with the FSA regulations on this.

If you are not directly responsible for the insurance you may still need to keep records as you may be required to provide details and access to the records particularly if the property is a residential one. Section 30a of the LTA 1985 brings into force a schedule to the Act 'Rights of Tenants With Respect to Insurance' This is dealt with in more detail in chapter 17 on insurance.

It is highly desirable to have a copy of each individual lease unless there is a very good reason for not having them. Copies of most commercial and residential leases are now available at a modest charge from HM Land Registry. Assuming that all leases are identical could prove a costly mistake.

6.3 What you must keep

In addition to the above details you will need to retain full accounting records including:

- all invoices;
- copies of any notices served;
- fire certificates and fire risk assessments;
- petroleum licences;
- health and safety assessments;
- insurance inspection reports;
- gas safety certificates;
- fire alarm test certificates; and
- electrical test certificates.

6.4 What else should you keep?

It is desirable to maintain detailed files on all tenants, guarantors (if any) and properties. You will frequently be called upon to answer questions about disputes and also deal with them – full and accurate records will make this task easier. Reading the file may also assist you in dealing with the parties and appreciating their concerns.

You should keep records of all licences granted and applications made. This is equally important for both commercial and residential management.

If a tenant obtains a guarantee for works then it is advisable to keep a copy with your records. It may be appropriate to make a claim at a later date and it may be helpful to be able to draw this to the attention of an assignee if things go wrong. In the residential sector Fenestration Self-Assessment Scheme (FENSA) and timber treatment guarantees are the most useful. If latent damage appears in the structure or in another demise as a result of works to a demise these records may enable you to pursue a claim on behalf of your clients.

You should keep records of major works and if possible the specifications and tender results. When cyclical works are due it should then be possible to assess the success of previous work and the contractors involved. Of course firms and methods do change over the years but an assessment of the successes and failures of the past may be very helpful in deciding the future course of action.

Long standing tenants will often remember what has gone wrong in the past and if you wish to gain their confidence proposing a repeat of what went wrong last time will be disastrous. Similarly if there was a big battle over a previous proposal, records will enable you to decide whether or not you really wish to go down that route again!

Even if not required for other purposes it is worthwhile maintaining records of Council Tax bandings and rateable values.

You will always need to have emergency contact numbers for tenants or under certain circumstances their relatives. These are particularly useful in case of flood or other serious incident and may be supplied as appropriate to the police when next of kin need to be contacted.

Obviously you can also use the tenants' telephone number if you need to jog their memory over accounts or to deal with other appropriate matters.

Where you are collecting a service charge from the occupier rather than the owner of the property you will need the owners address to deal with any serious breaches or non payment. It is best to warn them of any problems as soon as it becomes apparent that they are more than minor.

The new Land Registry rules which provide for three addresses should assist in tracing the owners of property interests but these can be out of date and involve making a search. It is preferable to have the information on file in any event.

While you may not be responsible for insurance it may be advantageous to keep a full set of records particularly if you have any intention of moving into the insurance field in the future.

6.5 Other records which you may be called upon to maintain

Company statutory books and registers

Many managing agents may not wish to have anything to do with maintaining company books and registers or helping out with their client's company affairs (it's understandable that they would not wish to take on the role of company secretary), but others will take a pragmatic approach and perform the tasks if not the role.

When it comes to maintaining the company register of members it may be that there is as much, if not more, work forwarding everything elsewhere than there is doing it. Maintenance of the register may also fit into the assignment procedure and if someone is being paid to do the job why should it not be you?

If you maintain the register of directors you will probably never have problems knowing who to send paperwork to.

When it comes to sending out AGM papers again your property management system can probably do this almost automatically and if your client management company lacks resources this could be an invaluable service to them. Although remember dealing with the AGM does not commit you to servicing the board.

Records of rent registrations

While regulated tenants are a dying breed they are nevertheless still quite plentiful and will continue for a good many years to come unless their status is abolished. The rent capping rules generally restrict increases to inflation plus 5 or 7.5 per cent unless works have been carried out which would increase the registered rent by 15 per cent over the existing registration.

This means that if a tenant, who is covered by the protection of the *Rent Act*, is moved into another property it will not be possible to increase the rent by more than the cap if there is an existing registration on that property even if it is 20 years old!

You might reasonably suggest that 15 per cent of a 20 year old rent would be very little but The Rent Service has been told to dispose of all paperwork over five years old except the actual registration. This means that it has disposed of all the survey reports which apply to the registration and will no longer hold records of the condition of the property. It may well occur to you that the service should have kept the records applying to the registration but such logic does not appear to have been followed!

The service has also disposed of paperwork concerning cancellation of registrations more than five years ago. In fairness it will have removed the properties from the register.

Due to the above it is very important to maintain accurate and detailed records. Wherever possible registered rents should be cancelled and once a protected tenant has moved out or died an application can be made to the rent officer for a cancellation certificate as long as two years have expired since the last registration. Cancellation certificates should be kept carefully.

Accurate and detailed records of all works to properties should be kept in order to justify the 15 per cent rule. Even though the registration may be ten years old and you may be convinced that considerable works have been carried out since the registration the Rent Officer and Rent Assessment Committee may not accept this without documentary proof. If they do not, however unreasonably, then your only appeal will lie with the High Court with its associated costs.

While it may at first be difficult to see how rent registrations can be relevant to service charge management unless you are also acting for the landlord, the increasing popularity of collective enfranchisement may lead to a few of these creeping in. The freeholder is entitled to insist that they are acquired as part of the enfranchisement. If you want to manage the building then you will doubtless have to agree to add these into the package. If you wish to move regulated tenants around for whatever reason you must be aware of the rent capping rules.

6.6 Importance of accuracy

Over the last 25 years we have moved from a situation where there was very little statutory intervention into property management, to one where it cannot be avoided. In the commercial sector this has focused on health and safety which means that accurate records and diaries must be kept to ensure that all requirements are complied with within the time limits laid down. If something goes wrong and the rules have not been complied with very dire consequences may result.

In the residential sector the list grows on an annual basis and includes:

- Accounts must be sent out within 18 months of expenditure being incurred or notice given otherwise costs may not be recovered (section 20B LTA 1985).
- Section 20 LTA 1985 notices must be served and the process complied with.
- Accounts must be provided in accordance with section 21 LTA 1985. This then sets out a timetable for providing access to records.
- Insurance details must be provided under section 30a LTA 1985. This also sets out a timetable for providing access to records.
- Lift inspections must take place.

Where lettings are concerned:

- gas safety certificates must be obtained at least every twelve months; and
- deposits are regulated.

6.7 Special requirements for houses in multiple occupation

If the property comes within the houses in multiple occupation (HMO) legislation *(and that includes flats in converted buildings)* the building may need a licence, unless they are more than two-thirds owner occupied or come up to the building regulations as they applied in June 1991 or as they applied when the conversion took place if at a later date.

This does not apply to a purpose-built block although it may to any part which has been subdivided.

It is a criminal offence not to have a licence for a HMO that requires one.

If only two people live in a property it cannot be a HMO.

Owner-occupied (subject to the comments below) means what it says not that a flat is simply held on a long lease.

Generally what most people would consider to be a HMO would not be a property to which the scope of this book would apply but converted blocks of flats clearly do fall within it.

The prescribed description of a HMO other than a converted block of flats is a property occupied by more than one household. It must consist of at least three stories and be occupied by at least five people. At present however it would appear that where converted blocks of flats are concerned the three storey and five people limits may not apply (see SI 2006/371).

This will leave you needing to ascertain:

- Is the property less than two-thirds 'owner-occupied'?
- Does the property come up to the applicable building regulations?
- Who is actually occupying it?

- Was the property converted?
- Was part of the property converted and if so which part? (A part of a building can be a HMO)
- Is subletting permitted under the terms of the lease?
- Who is liable to pay for improvements which, remember, may be required as a result of new statute?

The regulations are complicated and it remains to be seen whether or not some simplification will have to take place. Establishing the status of flats may be difficult as members of a household include cousins and owner-occupiers can take in up to two non-household members not to mention allowing any 'household member' to occupy in their own right and still be classed as owner-occupiers.

Interestingly the occupants usually have to occupy as their only or main residence, students occupying for the purposes of undertaking full time education being a notable exception.

If you manage converted property which does not come up to the appropriate building regulations then the need for accurate record keeping to work out whether or not it is a HMO is clearly of paramount importance. There are definitions of who is classed as living in a property and who forms part of a household. In fact as partners and relatives thereof including cousins are included, deciding whether or not a property is a HMO could prove very complicated.

What seems indisputable is that the detail and accuracy of records will need to be to a much higher standard than has been necessary in the past.

It is clear that if a converted block of flats comes into the HMO definition, you may either need to carry out a considerable amount of management work and incur substantial expense to obtain and comply with a licence or undertake improvements to bring it up to building regulation standards. In either case there will be weighty implications for the service charge.

Lessee addresses

As so many notices now have to be served on tenants it is essential that the addresses you hold are kept up to date. Indeed where certain converted blocks of flats are concerned it may be necessary to confirm whether the correspondence address is for accounting purposes or because the property is occupied by someone outside the lessees 'household'.

One very positive part of the CLRA 2002 as it applies to dealing with ground rent demands was the requirement for lessees to serve written notice of their address (in England and Wales). In the absence of such notice the property address must be used (CLRA 2002 section 166(6)). This does away with the favourite tactic of some disreputable 'commercial' residential lessees of never telling you where they move to and then arguing that they never received any bills or notices when the matter arrives in court.

With regards to section 166(6) it is somewhat amusing to note that the alternative address must be specifically in England and Wales. Presumably lessees living in other parts of the United Kingdom will need to make arrangements for their mail to be forwarded or dealt with by someone with an address in England and Wales – the rent is not recoverable until the notice is served neither can any interest be claimed for a period before it is correctly served.

The manager is in a happier position in that ground rent demands must be sent to the lessee at the property unless the lessee has served a notice stating an alternate address in England and Wales. You can of course send a copy to Scotland if you wish but you must then also send one to the property!

7

Setting service charge budgets

Accountability for service charges, budgetary control and certification of actual costs and accumulated reserves, are all matters which demand considerable attention.

This chapter covers the following topics:

- Budgets and on-account service charges
- Predicting the service charge costs
- Planned preventative maintenance
- Economy and efficiency
- The budgeting cycle
- Budget reports
- Industry standard list of account code descriptions
- Residential property

7.1 Budgets and on-account service charge

Nearly all modern leases will oblige the tenant to pay to the landlord a provisional sum of the tenant's proportion of the anticipated service charge calculated on an estimate of what the annual expenditure is likely to be for the forthcoming period. These on-account charges are usually payable in equal instalments (often quarterly) at the same time as the rent is paid.

In residential developments or smaller commercial properties an annual charge is more common especially where the range of services is less comprehensive.

Where one is required, the provision of an estimate of the anticipated service charge expenditure is very often a prerequisite to the tenant incurring any liability to make on-account payments. Subject to the strict wording of the occupational lease, if an estimate is not provided the tenants may not be liable to make any on-account payments until such time as an estimate has been provided.

It is therefore important to ensure that estimates are prepared and issued in accordance with the terms of the occupation lease and notified to tenants sufficiently in advance of the financial period in question to enable demands to be issued and ensure a continued cash flow to the landlord's service charge account to facilitate payment of invoices, etc.

The properly and proficiently prepared estimate of anticipated expenditure will also assist in monitoring and controlling expenditure which not only contributes to achieving stability of service charge expenditure year-on-year from the occupier's perspective but also provides an element of protection to the landlord from having to provide funds where tenants' quarterly advance contributions to service charges get out of step with expenditure or are inadequate to cover actual costs that are only balanced by the tenants' payments after the end of the service charge year.

An accurate budget will reduce the need to collect additional charges from tenants following reconciliation of the accounts for that year where actual expenditure exceeds the original estimate, but will also reduce the amount of credit balances due to tenants if actual expenditure falls below budget.

Contrary to popular belief, the property manager is not doing tenants a favour by handing money back to them at the end of the year (although this is often viewed as preferable to seeking to make a balancing charge).

As far as commercial property is concerned there is very often a real cost to the tenant in unnecessarily placing funds in the landlord's hands which might usefully have been used for its own business needs. Furthermore, some tenants view over budgeting as a way for the landlord to effectively obtain a free loan, particularly where the lease does not provide for all on-account payments to be held in an interest bearing account and for the interest earned to be credited to the benefit of the service charge.

The situation is somewhat different as regards the residential sector, the tenants may well prefer to have use of their money but many may have severe difficulty funding major or unforeseen expenditure at short notice. As the service charges are held in trust, the landlord cannot use the money for his or her own benefit. You should not significantly over budget but the budget should be robust.

The service charge budget is an estimate of anticipated expenditure, it is not a quotation. Budgeting is not an exact science and uncertainties and other unforeseen circumstances will often affect the eventual out-turn. However, what is important is that the property manager should be aware of circumstances which might affect the final actual position and should review actual expenditure against the original budget on a regular basis in order to manage expenditure, so far as possible, within the original budget set.

In addition to providing information to existing tenants to assist them with their own internal budgeting and cash flow, estimates of the anticipated service charge costs will be needed to facilitate first lettings of a newly completed scheme as well as when leases are due for renewal or at the time of rent reviews in older schemes.

It is possible to estimate with reasonable accuracy the cost of services in any building. In the case of a recently completed scheme, this task becomes easier as the building comes into use and the actual cost of operation and the particular requirements become evident. In the case of older schemes the day-to-day operational costs are more easily identified and estimated, however it is harder to predict major repairs and replacements as the plant and fabric wear out.

7.2 Predicting the service charge costs

This is particularly important in the majority of properties where the tenants pay a service charge in advance against cost estimates. In such cases the expenditure needs to be kept within those estimates if the landlord is not to have to provide funds to cover excess costs, albeit temporarily. Maintenance costs (e.g. external painting and decoration) recur on a regular basis but replacement items (e.g. the renewal of a flat roof) must be forecast well in advance. Other repairs may be completely unpredictable, such as fire or storm damage, but such would normally be covered by insurance.

Many tenants object to the wide variations in service charge costs year-on-year which can, in many circumstances, give rise to serious cash flow problems particularly when service charge costs increase dramatically in one year, say for example to take into account a major item of repair expenditure.

Where fixed price service contracts exist, accurate prediction of costs can often be achieved, but contracts that are due for renewal present a greater challenge. Ideally service contracts should be geared to expire near to the commencement of the service charge year and be re-tendered sufficiently in advance of the new financial period to enable an accurate estimate of likely costs to be prepared.

However, it can often be difficult to accurately predict all costs as it is not always practical or possible to obtain detailed quotes and tenders, particularly with regard to ad hoc maintenance and repair of the building and service installations. Furthermore, the non-cyclical and often unexpected occurrence of building defects can give rise to sudden and unpredictable fluctuations in total costs which will be a cause for concern to tenants

It is essential to predict costs, including provision for major repairs and replacements, and to produce budgets, preferably several years ahead, and attempt to work to them.

It is interesting to note that in some other countries reserve fund cash flow forecasts for residential property have to be certified on a regular basis concerning expenditure up to 50 years in advance. At first sight this may seem excessive but as items like lifts may have a 50 year life span such a comprehensive forecast will demonstrate that all relevant items have been considered.

7.3 Planned preventative maintenance

Many owners and managing agents now adopt a policy of planned preventative maintenance, which is generally considered to be best practice.

This involves regular surveys of the property to identify the anticipated life expectancy of plant and fabric, following which a comprehensive maintenance regime is worked up with the intention of extending the life of plant and fabric beyond the original expectancy. As part of this process, anticipated major repairs or replacements can more easily be predicted over a period of, say, five years. This planned preventative maintenance programme would be reviewed each year and works due to be carried out (maintenance, repair or replacement) are reflected in the annual service charge budget.

Planned preventative maintenance has the advantage that breakdowns or emergency repairs can be minimised through the planned maintenance of plant and equipment. Attending to emergency call-outs can be expensive, so the planned maintenance will have a positive effect upon the service charge and the accuracy of expenditure forecasting.

It is also possible to defer or bring forward certain works to achieve economies of scale. For instance works to replace a flat roof, necessitating expensive scaffolding, might be deferred until the latter part of one service charge year and combined with other works in the same location planned for the following year, so that the repair contract spans the two service charge years. This would result in a cost saving to the service charge by avoiding the need to scaffold the same location twice and also by taking advantage of any quantum discounts available in placing a larger repair contract.

Forecasts of expenditure must take into account not only the usual cost components but also the length of time the building is to operate each day. For instance, the introduction of Sunday Trading has extended the opening hours for many shopping centres which may result in plant and other equipment wearing out more quickly than was originally anticipated or that essential maintenance needs to be carried out in more anti-social hours at increased cost

A proper planned preventative maintenance regime would identify this and enable the property manager to take account of the changed circumstances to plan for the earlier than intended replacement or major repair of plant and equipment.

7.4 Economy and efficiency

A property manager needs to ensure that services are provided with due economy and efficiency and that costs are reasonable and proper. To that end the property manager must ensure that electricity and gas are paid for on the right tariff; that there is due regard to energy conservation and prevention of waste; that repairs are carried out at properly estimated and controlled costs; and that there is no extravagance in the standard of services provided. Conscientious control of expenditure engenders trust with tenant companies as (notwithstanding the lease wording and its interpretation as to the landlord's obligations) there is an overriding duty on the landlord to avoid extravagance and an unreasonable level of service costs and recovery.

Landlords in their efforts to contain service charges have been known to go to an extreme and allow buildings to become unkempt and shabby in order to contain costs. Where the service costs are only recoverable after they have been expended rather than in advance of the outlay, should the landlord decide that they cannot afford to properly finance the provision of adequate levels of services, standards will often decline and tenants become discontented.

In such circumstances the landlord might then be in breach of his or her obligations as set out in the occupational leases and therefore risks legal action to remedy the situation. Ultimately, remedial action will be required which may actually result in the need for greater expenditure than that which was hoped to have been avoided by deferring (or indeed ignoring) the problem in the first place.

Furthermore, in the case of repairs, if a building is allowed to deteriorate it invariably becomes more expensive, time consuming and disruptive to remedy the disrepair than if a proper repair had been initiated when the defects first came to light. If a landlord fails to comply with an obligation to repair, as a result of which additional repairs and damage is caused, the landlord will not generally be able to recover the additional costs under the service charge.

7.5 The budgeting cycle

The Code of Practice for *Service Charges in Commercial Property* requires owners to provide an estimate of likely service charge expenditure and appropriate explanatory commentary on it to the occupiers, together with their proportion of the costs, one month prior to the commencement of the service charge year.

Assuming a year-end of say 25 December, a programme for the service charge year might be as follows:

September/October (budget for forthcoming year)

- Obtain expenditure statement for preceding 9–10 months. Strip out non-recurring costs, and update regular costs for 12 months.

- Increase for estimated inflation for forthcoming year.

- Add anticipated non-recurring costs for forthcoming year.

- Obtain client approval/authorisation of the anticipated expenditure.

November/December

- Notify tenants of estimate for year.

- Demand new on-account service charges on 25 December (and each of three subsequent quarters).

February/March (reconciliation for previous year)

- Prepare expenditure statement for year-ending 24 December.

- Carry out service charge audit/reconciliation.

- Calculate balancing charges due from/to tenants and issue demands/credits with statement of expenditure.

September/October

- Obtain expenditure statement for preceding nine months, etc.

And so the cycle continues ...

7.6 Budget reports

Historically service charge reports have shown an almost infinite variety of style, format, account coding structure and referencing, and while there have been many examples of good reports unfortunately there are many examples of bad ones.

In the event of a change of ownership or of managing agents the absence of consistent industry standard report format and account coding structures has hitherto created significant problems in the comparison and benchmarking of costs property-to-property and when comparing costs year-on-year for the same property. This in turn has often led to significant problems and delays in the accurate reporting of expenditure to tenants and reconciliation of tenant accounts. It is not unusual for these delays to be measured in years rather than months.

Whether service charges are payable quarterly on account or annually in arrears, the tenants are entitled to know that their money is to be, or has been, well spent. An itemised statement in too much detail can provide a basis for unnecessary debate and a reason for a tenant to delay payment; but too little information will be equally unsatisfactory, provoking the tenant or his or her advisors to raise queries, if only to obtain reasonable satisfaction as to the composition of the costs involved.

In an effort to overcome these issues the Code of Practice for *Service Charges in Commercial Property* requires that budgets and actual expenditure accounts be issued with a report that provides:

(a) a reasonably comprehensive level of detail to enable occupiers to compare expenditure against estimated budget;
(b) explanations of significant individual costs and of variances from the previous year's budget/accounts;
(c) comparison against the previous two years' actual costs where appropriate;
(d) information on core matters critical to that account (e.g. levels of apportionment, contracts, report on tendering, etc.);
(e) the achieved and/or targeted measures of improved management performance (e.g. successes in delivering improved quality services and greater value for money);
(f) separately identified on-site management team costs;
(g) details and results of the last previous and forthcoming tendering exercise (occupiers will be advised of the contractors who are providing the services); and
(h) a statement detailing how income generated from operating the property (sometimes known as commercialisation or mall income) is dealt with and how shared services are charged, setting out how they impact

on the service charge and what reimbursement has been made to the service charge for these.

In many instances the recipient of the report may be the local tenant manager in the case of a large company or the principal in the case of smaller business. The local manager may well forward the report to a head office that would then deal with any queries or other issues. Service charge budget and actual expenditure reports may therefore be analysed by a variety of people with differing levels of knowledge concerning the lease terms and service charges generally.

As well as clearly identifying the property and the period to which the budget relates (this can be easily overlooked), it is considered to be best practice to include the following further information:

- an explanation of the service charge apportionment schedules and how the expenditure is apportioned to the schedules;
- an explanation of the basis of calculation of the tenant apportionments;
- an explanation of the basis of calculation of the management fee;
- a statement as to how VAT is treated; and
- a note of the person to whom any queries should be addressed. (This may seem to be self evidently the property manager but if the reports are issued centrally, queries are often directed to the accounts department or the property surveyor who may not be the ideal person to deal with a tenant query on say, security manning levels.)

Most important, however, is the incorporation of suitable explanatory notes. It should never be assumed that the ultimate recipient of the report will be as familiar with the property as you are. Local on-site managers can change with frustrating regularity and the financial director or head office service charge manager may be responsible for many other properties and may not therefore have a detailed knowledge of the subject property.

The explanatory notes should therefore be concise but should provide sufficient information and descriptions to reasonably satisfy a tenant that expenditure proposed or actually incurred has been wisely and reasonably considered.

It is now rarely acceptable to most tenants to be provided with a simple statement that 'costs have been held in line with last year's figures. For example, a property may have many contracts for the provision of various services expiring or subject to review and the tenants will wish to be satisfied that these have not been forgotten about, and what action is proposed. Re-negotiation of a contract will invariably have an impact upon the budget as this will present the opportunity to revise the specification if required to achieve, for instance, more cost efficient working methods. It also provides the opportunity to invite competitive tender prices with the ability, dependent upon market conditions, to negotiate a fixed price contract for a period of perhaps two or three years. It is reasonable therefore to expect the tenants to be informed of the assumptions that have been made in preparing the budget.

In addition to providing a breakdown of the estimated expenditure for the forthcoming year, a budget report should also include details of the current year's budget, anticipated outturn of actual costs against that budget, and details of the previous year's actual expenditure. This provides a general overview of the trend of expenditure year-on-year and is a useful barometer as to whether peaks and troughs of extra-ordinary expenditure are being successfully managed.

7.7 Industry standard list of account code descriptions

The Code of Practice for *Service Charges in Commercial Property* sets down a new standardised list of account code descriptions. The industry standard list of Account Codes is reproduced in appendix 2 of this book.

The new standardised account codes comprise seven major cost classes. These cost classes are divided into 22 cost categories which are further subdivided into detailed cost codes.

It is considered best practice to report expenditure to tenants at detailed cost code level, with a summary of the total costs under each cost category provided. However, for smaller properties or those with limited service charge expenditure (e.g. industrial sites) the minimum level of detail that would be acceptable would be to report at cost category. However, this should generally be regarded as an exception rather than the norm.

To maintain industry standards and to facilitate benchmark comparison, it is suggested that the cost class and cost category structure is not altered although the detailed cost codes are not intended to represent an exhaustive list, but are used for illustrative purposes only.

Owners and managing agents are therefore encouraged to include additional cost codes where this will facilitate greater transparency and clarity with regard to the expenditure incurred or proposed.

The commercial account coding structure

MANAGEMENT

1. Management fees

(See also chapter 22.)

In commercial properties management fees are often quoted as a percentage of actual service charge expenditure, very often ten per cent. Indeed, many leases will often state that the management fee is to be the actual cost of employing managing agents subject to a maximum of ten per cent of the total costs.

However, the Code of Practice requires that management fees reflect a reasonable price for the total cost of managing the provision and operation of the services.

The cost of rent collection is not usually regarded as a cost to the service charge but as a landlord non-recoverable cost (but see the terms of specific leases).

This total price will not be linked to a percentage of expenditure as such linkage is no longer felt to be appropriate and is a disincentive to the delivery of value for money.

The Code of Practice for *Service Charges in Commercial Property* further recommends the total price for the management service will be a fixed fee for a reasonable period of time (e.g. three years) and may be subject to indexing.

Best practice also requires that there will be transparency in the management fee charged, which will be reasonable for the work properly done in relation to the operation and management of the services and have due regard to the work necessary to fulfil the principles of the Code.

2. Accounting fees

These costs would include the fees and expenses for external audit of the service charge. This might also include other accounting fees and costs incurred by the owner and/or the managing agent and where separate from the management fee, should be clearly stated and properly reflected in the total cost of management. It may subject to the terms of the lease also include the accounting costs of a dedicated management company set up under the terms of the leases or as a RTM company under CLRA 2002.

3. Site management resources

The cost of administration and management of the building and all the services and functions in the common areas varies considerably between properties. Site management costs would include such matters as:

Staff costs

The total costs for staff include wages, national insurance and tax, statutory requirements, training, other appropriate benefits and the manager's administration charges, which should be declared.

Sufficient staffing of the right type and calibre should be provided to operate the services efficiently and cost effectively. However, as buildings have become more complex it is common, particularly in larger properties such as shopping centres, business parks and mixed-use schemes for the on-site staff to be of a very high calibre to the extent that they have in effect taken over responsibility for many roles and duties which have historically been viewed as the function of the managing agent. Indeed the on-site management team might be responsible for almost every aspect of the administration and management of the provision of the services and might even include accounts staff responsible for arranging payment of invoices, etc.

Furthermore, ensuring transparency in the management fee charged should reflect the roles and responsibilities of the on-site staff and the costs included within the service charge.

Notional rent

Many leases contain provision for the landlord to include a notional or deemed rent, which would originally have provided a financial return to the developer in defraying the costs of initial provision of the management offices. However, tenants generally object to the inclusion of notional rent as, in practice, the accommodation is either incapable of being used for any other purpose, and therefore has no intrinsic value other than as a location for the on-site management operation, or because the management offices comprise part of the original development which is a cost to be borne by the landlord.

In residential properties in particular it is common to charge a rent or notional rent if permitted on staff accommodation.

4. Health and safety, and environmental management

This would include consultancy fees and other costs associated with the provision and review of the owner's health and safety and other statutory requirements (*Control of Asbestos at Work Regulations* 2002, Disabled Access Audits, etc.).

UTILITIES

5. Electricity

This would comprise all energy costs in respect of the common areas and services: lifts, escalators, air-conditioning and heating, and so on, but excluding the cost of electricity consumption in respect of the occupied premises.

It is common practice for tenants to usually covenant in the lease to pay the cost of all electricity consumption in respect of the demised premises direct to the electricity supplier. Alternatively, where the premises are not separately metered the tenant would covenant to reimburse the landlord a proportion of the electricity charges appropriate to the demised premises on demand and outside of the service charge.

However, subject to the terms of the lease, where direct energy costs are included under the service charge these should be shown under a separate cost heading distinct from the costs of the common parts and landlord's services.

This heading would also include consultancy and procurement fees for negotiating electricity supply contract and auditing of energy consumption

6. Gas

As electricity.

7. Fuel Oil (Heating)

As electricity.

8. Water

As electricity.

SOFT SERVICES

9. Security

Security costs would not only include the salaries and on-costs of either direct or contracted labour but also the cost of maintenance and repair of security equipment such as closed-circuit television, alarms, security radios, etc. together with the cost of repairs and maintenance to the security control room and rest rooms if separate from the on-site property management offices.

10. Cleaning and environmental

This would include, internal, external and window cleanings, maintenance and repair of equipment, provision of cleaning materials, hygiene services, toiletries and other consumables, refuse removal, pest control, and interior planting and external landscape maintenance costs.

11. Marketing and promotions

Marketing and promotions costs usually relate principally to shopping centres, or retail and leisure parks. For further advice and guidance refer to A Good Practice Guide – Shopping Centre Marketing and Promotions which is a publication endorsed by BCSC.

HARD SERVICES

12. Mechanical and electrical services

Planned maintenance of the owners mechanical and electrical services, fire protection, emergency lighting and other specialist life safety systems, including auditing the quality of maintenance works, the condition of plant, and health and safety compliance.

13. Lifts and escalators

Planned maintenance and repair of common parts' passenger and goods lifts and escalators including auditing of the quality of maintenance works, the condition of plant and health and safety compliance.

14. Suspended access equipment

Planned maintenance and repair of all forms of high-level access equipment maintenance, i.e. latchway, eye-bolt, fall address and cradles, including auditing the quality of maintenance works, the condition of plant and health and safety compliance.

15. Fabric repairs and maintenance

Repair, maintenance and decoration of the structure, external and internal building fabric, common parts and retained areas.

INCOME

16. Interest

Interest received on service charge monies held within owner's or agent's bank account.

17. Income from commercialisation

In addition to rents collected in respect of occupational leases, some properties, e.g. shopping centres, retail and leisure parks, might also generate income from a number of sources such as public telephones, promotional space and various licences granted in respect of other activities within the common parts. The treatment of this income is a subject of considerable variance from property to property, landlord to landlord.

The landlord will usually seek to optimise the income from his or her investment. However tenants object to income generated from the common parts being retained by the landlord when it is the tenants who pay for the cleaning, lighting and other costs associated with these areas.

It is important to maintain records of income receipts from different sources and activities as the nature of the activity would generally indicate whether the landlord or the tenants should receive the benefit of the income.

Any income derived from the provision of a service or activity, the cost of which would normally fall to the service charge, should be treated as a service charge credit (e.g. income from public telephones, toilet vending machines, photocopy and fax reimbursements etc.). Similarly, income derived from promotional activity would normally be credited to the promotional expenditure budget.

However, if the use of the space is of a permanent or semi-permanent nature (e.g. barrows or kiosks located within the malls) it is common practice for the landlord to retain the income as rent and the space should be included in the service charge apportionment matrix. Alternatively, a sum should be credited to the service charge to reflect a contribution towards the benefit of the services provided.

One aspect that does not seem to be universally applied is the point at which income is applied to the service charge. In many instances, income is credited against expenditure and the net figure shown in the service charge account. This can then result in some strange anomalies in that a large credit within the service charge would reduce the management fee due to the managing agents when there might be considerable involvement in managing the accounts – in effect the managing agents are paying the tenants.

Income should therefore be credited to the service charge after calculation of the management fee. In this way not only is the anomaly referred to above avoided, but the costs and income receipts are shown separately in the service charge account which is considered to be good accounting practice.

18. Insurance

The cost of insurance against fire, special perils and loss of rent, not only of the main building and common areas but also of the premises let, may be included in the service charge. However, unlike many other costs the insurance premium would usually be payable annually at renewal, rather than monthly or quarterly.

As the insurance premium can constitute a major item of expenditure, the landlord can experience cash flow problems in recovering the cost over the period of the service charge year. Therefore the recovery of the building insurance premium is often dealt with outside the service charge and the lease will make provision for recovery of insurance premiums as an additional rent.

19. Engineering insurance

engineering;

engineering inspections; and

vehicles.

20. All risks insurance cover

building insurance;

loss of rent insurance;

employers liability;

public and property owner's liability;

landlords contents; and

plate glass.

21. Terrorism insurance

terrorism.

EXCEPTIONAL EXPENDITURE

22. Major works

The replacement of fabric, plant and equipment can involve substantial expenditure beyond that which might be regarded as 'regular' day-to-day maintenance and repair.

The law defining what constitutes repair, renewal, replacement or improvement is extensive and it will often become a matter of debate and lease interpretation as to the point at which such expenditure can be included within the service charge.

It is generally accepted that service charge costs will usually include the reasonable costs of maintenance repair and replacement (where beyond economical repair) of fabric, plant, equipment and materials. Such costs may include enhancement where such expenditure can be justified following the analysis of reasonable options and alternatives.

23. Forward funding

sinking funds;

reserve funds; and

depreciation charges.

7.8 Residential property

CLRA 2002 made provision for a standard form of accounts and a great deal of consultation has taken place on this. At the end of the day the above commercial code does not apply to the residential sector and it will be necessary to tailor budgets to tie in with any prescribed form of accounts. While it is necessary to provide explanations with the budget, this needs to be in a form which can be readily understood by the tenants concerned. It should not be over complicated nor over simplified.

8

Apportionment of the service charge

The apportionment of the service charge is an issue that requires considerable thought and attention. For older properties, the basis and method should, whenever possible, be reviewed to ensure that the resultant apportionment of the service charge expenditure is fair and equitable.

Prospective purchasers of a multi-occupied building for which a service charge is in place are advised, as part of the due diligence process prior to completion, to undertake a review of the service charge. Particularly attention should be given to the method and basis of apportionment to ensure that the service charge has historically been calculated in accordance with the terms of the lease and that the method and basis of apportionment of the service charge is known and understood.

Similarly, managing agents taking on a new management instruction should, as a matter of course fully review the basis and methodology for calculating the service charge apportionments and should ensure that all appropriate and requisite information is made available (for example an agreed and up to date schedule of floor areas, etc.).

This chapter covers the following topics:

- Basic principles
- Benefit and use
- Common methods of apportionment
- Apportionment schedules

8.1 Basic principles

Whatever basis of apportionment is used, it must be demonstrably fair and reasonable to ensure that individual tenants bear an appropriate, fair and reasonable proportion of the total service charge expenditure that reflects the benefit of the services enjoyed. Landlords should apply the method and basis of apportionment consistently throughout the property having regard to the physical size, nature of use, and benefits to and use by occupiers.

From the landlord's perspective, the basis of apportionment should enable 100 per cent recovery of the costs incurred in carrying out works and in providing services to the common areas and facilities of the building. However, the landlord should bear the cost of the proportion of the service charge relating to void or unlet units, any concessions given to any one occupier and the proportion attributable to his or her own use of the property.

But, there is no general rule that the tenants of a building should be treated in a consistent manner. Each lease is an individual contract and the terms of one contract cannot determine, override or influence the terms of another.

8.2 Benefit and use

In assessing a 'fair' apportionment of the service charge, reference should be made to the benefit received by the tenants from the provision of a facility or service and not necessarily its use.

A tenant located on the first floor of an office block may not actually 'use' the lift provided for the building, as it may be more convenient to use the stairs but the tenant nevertheless has the benefit of the lift service should it be required (e.g. for use by a disabled member of staff or visitor).

Similarly, a tenant on the ground floor of a multi-storey building would benefit from the protection afforded by the roof to the building as a whole. The tenant of the ground floor would therefore derive equal benefit from the fact that the roof is maintained in good repair to prevent water ingress – notwithstanding that the tenant of the top floor may be the first to experience problems should the roof fail.

8.3 Common methods of apportionment

Leases vary in the manner by which they define or provide for the ascertaining of each individual tenant's proportion of the total service charge costs to the building.

Most modern commercial leases will provide for the tenant's share of the service charge to be: '... a fair and reasonable proportion as determined from time to time by the landlords' surveyor ...' Frequently the lease will also include reference to the primary method or basis of apportionment to be used, for instance, by including additional wording such as: '... having regard to the proportion which the lettable floor area of the Premises bears to the aggregate lettable floor area of the building ...'

A fair and reasonable basis of determining the service charge apportionments for individual tenants has the benefit of providing flexibility and, for the landlord, full recovery. Where the lease does not make reference to the primary method by which the tenant apportionments are to be calculated, the landlord's surveyor will be free to use whatever method or basis of apportionment that he or she feels would produce a 'fair and reasonable' allocation of the service charge.

But, unless coupled with a statement as to how the tenant's apportionment is to be calculated, uncertainty and disputes can often arise, although 'fair and reasonable' places an onus on the landlord to ensure that no one tenant is disadvantaged against the others.

Alternatively, the lease might provide for the service charge to be based on a fixed amount or fixed percentage of the costs, usually agreed as part of the original lease negotiations, or such other basis of apportionment as the parties to the contract feel appropriate.

The most common methods of apportionment are:

1   a fixed or indexed amount;
2   a fixed percentage;
3   rateable value;
4   floor area; and
5   weighted floor area.

Apportionments for residential properties are generally restricted to fixed and sometimes variable percentages. If these are not stated specifically in the leases the Leasehold Valuation Tribunal may be asked to make a determination

A *fixed or indexed amount*

These are fairly self-explanatory – the amount the tenant will pay of the overall service charge is fixed at the time the lease is granted. The charge may be fixed for the whole term or may be subject to an annual indexed increase in accordance with, for example, the retail price index (RPI). Similarly, the tenant may covenant to pay a fair and reasonable proportion of the service charge but which might be subject to a maximum amount of cap. This cap might itself be subject to annual indexation.

Advantages

This method provides certainty for both landlord and tenant, is simple and when the fixed sum is not subject to indexation, results in no calculation costs. Even if subject to indexation, the calculation is a relatively simple exercise.

The fixed amount may be advantageous for short leases where costs are unlikely to vary significantly or where a limited scope of services is to be provided with little risk of unforeseen expenditure.

Disadvantages/problem areas

A fixed amount is inflexible and can give rise to under or over recovery in the event that the actual cost of providing the common services and facilities varies from the fixed amount agreed.

Where the fixed amount is subject to indexation and is not stated in the lease to be a cap on the tenant's liability, the actual amount payable could exceed or fall short of the actual cost of providing the services in the event that actual costs do not vary in line with the index.

A *fixed percentage*

As above, these are fairly self-explanatory. The percentage that the tenant will pay of the overall service charge costs is fixed at the time the lease is granted.

Advantages

The fixed percentage offers certainty and simplicity but is inflexible and should only be used where the landlord's premises are unlikely to vary. Provision is therefore often included within the lease to review the fixed percentage in the event that the building is substantially altered or extended.

Disadvantages/problem areas

It is not uncommon for fixed percentages to be agreed as part of the lease negotiations. As a consequence, and unless calculated by reference to a specific basis of apportionment, the fixed percentage can give rise to under or over recovery. Situations do exist where the sum of the fixed percentages included in the various leases add up to more than 100 per cent.

While there is nothing to prevent a landlord from granting leases which stipulate fixed percentages or amounts that aggregate to more than 100 per cent, the basic principle that the landlord should not profit from the provision of services suggests that such practice is at best immoral and is therefore not in accordance with the principles of good estate management.

Rateable value apportionment

The lease may state that the tenant's proportion of the service charge is to be calculated by reference to the proportion that the rateable value of the demised premises bears to the total rateable value of the lettable parts of the building (i.e. excluding common areas and management accommodation).

The lease will usually provide for recalculation as rateable values change with each rating revaluation.

Advantages

Rateable values can be readily ascertained and are fixed by a third party. This means that where the lease is otherwise silent, and does not refer to a requirement that the apportionment should be fair and reasonable, there is limited scope to dispute the data used to apportion the service charge, unlike other methods.

As rateable values are based on valuation principles, they will often reflect a quantum reduction for large space users. The rateable value of a small shop will not be calculated at the same rate per square metre as a department store and therefore rateable value calculations would result in a discounted apportionment for larger premises in a similar manner to weighted floor area (see page 87).

Disadvantages/problem areas

Over a number of years, rateable values may be changed with the tenant having the right to appeal against the assessment. Technically speaking, and unless the lease makes specific provision to the contrary, the tenant's service charge apportionment would need to be checked against the rating list and recalculated as appropriate every time an invoice was paid.

Rating appeals can also take many years to be resolved which could result in the need to recalculate the tenant's service charge apportionment for previous years. It therefore follows that the landlord would need to recalculate the service charge apportionments for all other tenants, and recover further balancing charges. This would occur every time an individual tenant succeeds in appealing a ratings value and is potentially an administrative nightmare.

Many landlords have adopted a policy of using only the rateable values that exist in the rating list at the time of calculating the service charge. Any subsequent variations to the list would only be used for calculating apportionments for future years. Many tenants have accepted this as a common sense approach and it is generally considered to be in accordance with best practice.

Rateable values also reflect a number of factors including location. For instance otherwise identical shop units in a shopping centre but located in prime and secondary positions will have different rateable values, which would result in the calculation of differing apportionments even though the benefit of the provision of the services would in theory be the same.

Part V of the *Local Government Planning and Land Act* 1980 abolished the statutory requirement for revision of rateable values for residential properties. Therefore in respect of mixed-use developments that include a residential element it is no longer possible to compare rateable values at a consistent valuation date. Rateable value apportionments for residential properties are becoming increasingly rare while for mixed-use properties that include a residential element, apportionment of the service charge based on rateable value have become manifestly erroneous.

Floor area apportionment

The standard floor area method of apportionment is simply the ratio that the lettable area of the demise bears to the total or aggregate of the lettable parts of the building. Leases will often specify the basis of measurement to be used, e.g. net internal or gross internal floor area, measured in accordance with the *RICS Code of Measuring Practice*.

The *RICS Code of Measuring Practice* sets out definitions relating to the measurement of buildings and their recommended applications. With regard to the calculation of service charges, the main definitions are as follows:

Definition	Application
Gross Internal Area (GIA)	Industrial and warehouses (including ancillary offices)
Gross External Area (GEA)	Alternatively applied to industrial and warehouses (including ancillary offices)
Net Internal Area (NIA)	Offices and shops

Advantages

This is the most common method of apportionment used and is in most circumstances, the fairest. Floor area apportionment rarely gives rise to problems when applied in circumstances where the extent of benefit of the provision of the services would, all things be equal, be considered constant, e.g. offices.

Disadvantages / problem areas

Unless the lease specifies what floor area is to be used (e.g. GIA or NIA) inaccurate unfair apportionment might result if, for example, both GIA and NIA are used. For instance, standard shops are usually measured for rental valuation purposes on the basis of NIA whereas larger premises such as department stores will often be measured on the basis of GIA.

Where the lease does not make reference to the basis of measurement to be used, but instead refers only to the proportion that the 'lettable' area of the demise bears to the total 'lettable' area of the property, inequity or an unintended result may be produced where the *RICS Code of Measurement Practice* and convention specifies alternative methods of measurement for different types of use. This can be particularly crucial for mixed-use developments where there might be a variety of retail, office, leisure and residential use.

It is therefore essential that floor area records kept by landlords or managing agents clearly distinguish the basis of measurement and, if these are different, that separate consistent floor area measurements are used for the purposes of calculating tenant service charge apportionments.

It is not unheard of for the majority of leases granted in respect of a shopping centre to specify apportionment of the service charge based on NIA whereas the lease of the anchor store specifies apportionment based on GIA.

In these circumstances two entirely separate calculations would be required; one for the majority of the tenants based on NIA to include the NIA of the anchor store, and another in respect of the anchor store based on GIA using only GIAs for all units within the scheme.

Not only is this administratively complex it is extremely unlikely that 100 per cent recovery would be achieved. Depending upon the ratio of gross to net areas and the size of the anchor store compared to the remainder of the scheme, an under or over recovery of the service charge would result.

Floor areas can often 'vary' between rent reviews. Tenants may carry out physical alterations that affect the lettable floor area of the demised premises. Therefore, tenant apportionments may alter over time even though the building has not itself been physically altered.

The issue of tenant alterations and the effect these would have on the calculation of the apportionment of the service charge can also give rise to an unusual situation.

For example, a tenant of a retail park decides to add a mezzanine floor within their premises. This is an alteration that would require the landlord's consent, which is duly obtained, and the licence provides that the tenant's improvement is to be disregarded at rent review.

However, modern leases will usually describe the demised premises and the landlord's property as including any improvements and alterations. Therefore, the new mezzanine floor would be included within the definitions of the demised premises and within the definition of the aggregate lettable space for the property.

As a result, the net internal or gross internal area of the demised premises will increase as will the total lettable floor area for the property.

The tenant's service charge apportionment, if calculated on the basis of net or gross Internal floor area, would therefore increase while the apportionment in respect of other premises that are not similarly altered, would decrease.

Furthermore, if the service charge has historically been calculated on the basis of a fixed percentage and the lease does not provide for the fixed percentage to be adjusted as a result of tenant alterations, the tenant's service charge proportion (and that of other tenants) would not alter.

Therefore, when dealing with alterations to premises, particularly where these require the prior consent or approval of the landlord, consideration should always be given to the potential impact upon the calculation of the service charge to ensure that the apportionment continues to be fair and reasonable, and in accordance with the terms of the leases.

In carrying out the improvement works the tenant could therefore incur an additional service charge liability, which might not necessarily have been envisaged.

Weighted floor area apportionment

In many larger shopping centres and mixed-use developments a 'weighted floor area' formula is common to reflect the different costs involved in servicing different sized units and the varying benefit received of the services and facilities provided between different uses.

Thus, a 2,000m^2 unit will not cost ten times that of a 200m^2 unit, but a 200m^2 unit may cost twice that of a 100m^2 unit.

A 'weighted floor area' apportionment will discount the percentage the tenant will pay over a certain size in an effort to reflect the benefit of the services provided. The floor area is divided into bands with a progressive discount – conceptually this is a similar idea to the zoning of shops for rental purposes.

The first	300 m²	@ 100 per cent
The next	300 m²	@ 80 per cent
The next	400 m²	@ 60 per cent
The next	500 m²	@ 50 per cent
The next	1,000 m²	@ 40 per cent
Excess over	2,500 m²	@ 30 per cent

In the example above a 1,000m² unit will have a weighted floor area of 720m², i.e. (300 x 100 per cent) + (300 x 80 per cent) + (400 x 60 per cent), whereas a 10,000m² unit will have a weighted area of 3,620m². Therefore although ten times larger in floor area terms, the 10,000m² unit will pay approximately five times the service charge of the smaller unit.

A simple example of a weighted floor area calculation, with the resultant relative rates per m² is set out below.

	Unweighted		Weighted			
	Floor area (m²)	per cent	Floor area (m²)	per cent	Total Service Charge (£)	Rate per m² (£)
Department store	7,500	41.75	2,870	26.23	152,088.97	20.28
LSU	1,950	10.86	1,150	10.51	60,941.57	31.25
LSU	1,530	8.52	982	8.97	52,038.80	34.01
LSU	1,725	9.60	1,060	9.69	56,172.23	32.56
MSU	740	4.12	624	5.70	33,067.43	44.69
MSU	970	5.40	762	6.96	40,380.42	41.63
MSU	455	2.53	424	3.87	22,468.89	49.38
MSU	403	2.24	382	3.49	20,264.40	50.28
Standard Unit	165	0.92	165	1.51	8,743.79	52.99

Standard Unit	151	0.84	151	1.38	8,001.89	52.99
Standard Unit	158	0.88	158	1.44	8,372.84	52.99
Standard Unit	175	0.97	175	1.60	9,273.72	52.99
Standard Unit	100	0.56	100	0.91	5,299.27	52.99
Standard Unit	150	0.84	150	1.37	7,948.90	52.99
Standard Unit	150	0.84	150	1.37	7,948.90	52.99
Standard Unit	160	0.89	160	1.46	8,478.83	52.99
Standard Unit	200	1.11	200	1.83	10,598.53	52.99
Standard Unit	100	0.56	100	0.91	5,299.27	52.99
Standard Unit	125	0.70	125	1.14	6,624.08	52.99
Standard Unit	125	0.70	125	1.14	6,624.08	52.99
Standard Unit	150	0.84	150	1.37	7,948.90	52.99
Standard Unit	150	0.84	150	1.37	7,948.90	52.99
Standard Unit	175	0.97	175	1.60	9,273.72	52.99
Standard Unit	175	0.97	175	1.60	9,273.72	52.99
Standard Unit	200	1.11	200	1.83	10,598.53	52.99
Standard Unit	30	0.17	30	0.27	1,589.78	52.99
Standard Unit	25	0.14	25	0.23	1,324.82	52.99
Standard Unit	25	0.14	25	0.23	1,324.82	52.99
	17,962	100	10,943	100	579,920	32.29

In this simplified example, the overall service charge rate for the scheme is £32.29 per m^2 (£3 per ft^2) although the actual service charges payable vary from between £20.28 per m^2 (£1.88 per ft^2) for the department store anchor and £52.99 per m^2 (£4.92 per ft^2) for the standard units.

In a similar way, basement and upper floors accommodation, used possibly for storage or staff rooms, can be 'weighted', say by dividing the floor area by a factor of two, to reflect the benefit derived from the services as distinct from the ground floor retail space.

A weighted floor area basis of apportionment might also be used to reflect varying benefit based on hours of use. For instance, the floor area of premises used as a call centre 24 hours a day, 7 days a week (168 hours per week) might be 'weighted' to reflect the benefit of the services provided compared with other premises used only during 'normal' business hours (say 08.00–18.30 Monday to Friday and 09.00–12.30 Saturdays = 56 hours per week). In this example, the floor area for the call centre would be 'weighted' by 300 per cent to reflect that the premises are used for three times longer than the other premises within the building.

However, a weighted calculation based on hours of use might only apply to certain costs and services. Utilities, consumables such as toilet requisites, maintenance of lifts, and heating equipment, etc. might be said to increase as a direct result of actual usage, whereas the cost of say building maintenance and repair might not be influenced by abnormal use. Therefore in such instances it may not be appropriate to apply the weighting to all cost categories.

Advantages

Weighted floor areas enable costs to be apportioned to reflect the perceived benefit derived from the services and facilities provided.

Disadvantages

Weighted floor areas are commonly used to provide a discount to an anchor tenant to reflect the benefit the anchor tenant brings to the shopping centre. Such weightings must be approached with a degree of caution as in some cases the weighting is in fact calculated to provide the anchor store with a 'concession', with the purpose being to spread the cost of the concession amongst the remaining tenants.

Best practice prescribes that the owner should meet the cost of any special concession given by an owner to any one occupier.

Calculating weighted floor area apportionments

If based on hours of use, as above, the floor area weightings applied would usually be self evident and based on a subjective or actual assessment of benefit and use.

However, in determining a basis of a progressive discount for size, a standard industry formula for calculating weighted floor area apportionments does not exist. The appropriate weighting will vary dependent upon the size of the development and the relationship between the number and relative sizes of individual units and in many circumstances the bandings and discounts applicable will be a result of trial and error.

Various weighted floor area permutations will be tried in an effort to calculate levels of service charge for small, medium and large space users that achieves a fair and reasonable apportionment of the service charge between tenants.

However, it can be difficult to justify a weighted floor area which has been arrived at on the basis of trial and error as this will often be viewed as a subjective opinion. In many circumstances a more objective analytical approach is sometimes preferred and necessary.

The rateable value approach

While for the various reasons outlined rateable values are not recommended as a basis for the ongoing annual apportionment of the service charge, they are independently assessed and being based on valuation principles will often reflect a quantum reduction for size.

Rateable values might also provide a reasonable benchmark for the relative apportionments between different use types.

Rateable values (or for a new development a reasonable appraisal of likely rateable values) might be used as a 'first cut' in formulating weighted floor area bandings and progressive discount percentages.

An exact correlation between a rateable value apportionment and a weighted floor area formula is rarely possible as rateable values are also affected by a number of different factors such as location, layout, etc., but a weighted floor area formula that results in an approximation of the ratios between differing sizes of unit produced by a comparison of rateable values might arguably be a more objective calculation than one obtained simply through trial and error.

For instance, if in the example above the department store anchor tenant has an anticipated rateable value which equates to 25 per cent of the total anticipated rateable value for the scheme, the bandings used for the calculation of the weighted floor area apportionment might therefore seem to be reasonable.

Once established, the weighted floor area percentages would then be used for the ongoing annual apportionment of the service charge between tenants irrespective of any subsequent changes of alterations to the actual rateable values.

The pedestrian flow approach

This approach might be useful for mixed-use schemes particularly in the case of estate service charges where the 'benefit' of the services enjoyed by different user types is more difficult to assess

For instance, let us assume a scheme that includes equal total floor areas of residential, retail, leisure and office space and that all tenants have the shared benefit of a quality external managed environment comprising landscaping, roadways, pedestrian areas and streetscape, etc.

Retail and leisure, as commercial operators, will encourage as many customers to the site as possible. These customers, as well as the tenants' own staff will benefit from the external managed environment.

The staff and visitors to the offices element will also benefit as will the residential tenants and their visitors. But, the number of people enjoying the benefit of the services provided by the landlord on providing a quality external environment will not be directly relative to the floor area occupied.

While some assumptions will have to be made in order to achieve what would be regarded as a fair and reasonable apportionment of the costs, sufficient analysis and data is available which should enable an assessment of the likely pedestrian flow generated by each use type, and which can then be used to objectively calculate a weighted floor area formula.

For example, a 115,000m^2 mixed-use scheme comprises 50,000m^2 residential, 40,000m^2 retail, 10,000m^2 office and 15,000m^2 leisure space.

Anticipated annual pedestrian flow generated by each use type is estimated as follows:

Residential	980,000
Retail	13,780,000
Offices	940,000
Leisure	2,260,000
	17,960,000

Therefore, based on the assessment of anticipated pedestrian flow, the following weighted floor area apportionment would apply:

	Pedestrian Flow	per cent	Weighting per cent	Floor Area (m²)	Unweighted per cent	Weighted Floor Area (m²)	Weighted per cent
Residential	980,000	5.46	7.51	50,000	43.48	3,755	8
Retail	13,780,000	76.73	100	40,000	34.78	40,000	85.30
Offices	940,000	5.23	6.82	10,000	8.70	682	1.45
Leisure	2,260,000	12.58	16.40	15,000	13.04	2,460	5.25
	17,960,000	100.00		115,000	100.00	46,897	100.00

Therefore, the residential element, while comprising over 44 per cent of the floor area of the scheme would contribute approximately seven per cent of the estate service charge, while the retail element, comprising approximately 35 per cent of the scheme in terms of floor area, might bear 86 per cent of the total costs.

As with rateable values, once the relative weighted floor area percentages have been established these would then be used for the ongoing annual apportionment of the service charge between tenants.

When is a weighted floor area apportionment not a weighted floor area apportionment?

Smaller space users who pay a higher rate per square foot compared with larger space users that receive the benefit of a discounted service charge to reflect the size of the demised premises, will very often view a weighted floor area apportionment simply as a device to provide larger tenants (usually the anchor tenant of a shopping centre scheme) with a concessionary service charge discount, for which the tenants effectively pay, rather than viewing the weighted floor area apportionment as a bona fide attempt to achieve a fair and reasonable apportionment of the costs of providing the services.

This raises the 'chicken and egg' question – which came first, the weighted floor area apportionment of the service charge or the 'concession' given to the anchor tenant?

Whether a concession was first given to a large space user and the weighted floor area formula calculated in order to achieve 100 per cent recovery for the landlord can very often be easily identified.

If the tenant service charge contributions are calculated by first deducting the contributions received from the anchor tenant(s) from the service charge costs, with the balance of expenditure then apportioned between the remaining tenants, this is usually a clear indication that the level of service charge payable by the anchor tenant(s) is at a concessionary rate. This would not be regarded as a properly constituted weighted formula as the anchor tenant's contribution is unlikely to have been calculated based on a consistent formula, or might be calculated excluding certain heads of expenditure. If this were not the case why calculate the apportionments for the remaining tenants in this way?

Other ways to demonstrate whether the weighted floor area apportionment calculation exists simply to provide 100 per cent recovery of the service charge costs for the landlord having given a concessionary discount to certain tenants is to firstly check whether the discounted rate for each of the major tenants is calculated on a similar basis. If not, this would be another clear indication that the service charge contribution was an item negotiated as part of the original lease terms.

However, many landlords are often reluctant to provide details of how the service charge apportionments for anchor stores have been calculated and it can therefore be difficult to verify this.

Similarly, the weighted floor area apportionment basis should be timeless. If properly constituted and applied, the formula will enable all tenant apportionments to be readily re-calculated in the event of any significant alteration or extension of the property.

For instance, if a large space user vacated the premises which were then subdivided into individual standard sized units it should be possible to recalculate all tenants' apportionments consistently. In such circumstances where the total weighted floor area is altered, the percentage of the service charge payable by the other large space units would also change.

Where the weighted floor area formula is not properly constituted and applied to all occupiers the owner should meet the cost of the concession given. A reasonable and fairly administered weighting formula for apportionment of the service charge cannot usually be considered a concession.

There is no such thing as a standard industry formula for calculating weighted floor area apportionments.

8.4 Apportionment schedules

In many cases, particularly in mixed-use buildings not all the tenants in the building will enjoy the benefit of the landlord's services to the same extent. For example, offices located above a parade of shops may benefit from a full range of services including a lift and an independent central heating system while the shops may only benefit from general repairs and maintenance to the exterior of the property and benefit from other common services and facilities such as refuse disposal, maintenance of the common fire alarm system, etc.

However, even in single-use properties, ground floor tenants may not pay for a lift even when deliveries are made via the basement using it, and tenants who do not have access to common parts may or may not pay for their upkeep – for example only certain tenants may have the use of car parking or garage space. Furthermore, the lease itself might also dictate that only particular tenants are to be responsible for the payment of certain costs.

For larger mixed-use buildings the situation may be made even more complex with different user groups using the building at different times and for different periods. For example office tenants might use their premises only during normal office hours, retail tenants during the hours of 9.00–18.00 Monday to Saturdays (with additional but reduced hours on Sunday) whereas leisure uses such as restaurants/bars, cinemas, etc. might be open for trade at a later time but would remain open for considerably extended periods.

Such extended hours of use might result in additional costs in the provision of services, which might not otherwise have been necessary had it not been for the nature and type of extended hours. For instance, while the property might benefit from 24-hour security, additional and enhanced security arrangements might be required during the extended hours of opening for the restaurants and bars and it would not be reasonable for the other retail and office tenants to bear a proportion of such additional costs.

However, the extent to which an occupier should contribute towards the cost of a particular service is not always a matter of **use** of the service or facility, but of the **benefit** that the tenant receives of the service or facility provided. This is often distinct from the use or occupation of premises.

Premises that are connected to a centralised heating and air-conditioning system but which are vacant would not **use** the heating and air-conditioning to the same extent as occupied premises but would still have the **benefit** of the service.

If a majority of tenants neither used nor indeed required the provision of a particular service or facility the landlord should, in the interests of good estate management, consider discontinuing the service following appropriate consultation with the tenants. However, there is no established principle whereby a tenant can arbitrarily choose to cease using a particular common facility or service and sustain that it henceforth has no liability to pay a proportion of the costs.

For the various reasons mentioned above it may be necessary to divide the service charge expenditure into separate parts, (or Schedules) with the costs being apportioned between tenants according to use/benefit.

In the example opposite the costs of services and facilities common to all tenants would be apportioned, based on floor area under Schedule 1.

Schedule 2 would provide for the apportionment of those costs relating to the office tenants only (e.g. heating the demised premises, the provision of a lift service, lighting and maintenance of common parts, etc).

Schedule 3 would provide for the apportionment of the enhanced security costs resulting from the restaurant/bars' extended hours of opening.

		Schedule 1	Schedule 2	Schedule 3
Unit Description	**Floor Area (m²)**	**All Tenants (%)**	**Offices only (%)**	**Extended hours security (%)**
Shop 1	100	4.44		
Shop 2	100	4.44		
Shop 3 (Bar)	200	8.89		44.44
Shop 4 (Restaurant)	250	11.11		55.56
First Floor	400	17.78	25.0	
Part Second Floor	160	7.11	10.0	
Part Second Floor	240	10.67	15.0	
Third Floor	400	17.78	25.0	
Fourth Floor	400	17.78	25.0	
Total	**2,250**	**100**	**100**	**100**

This is a simple example and the apportionment matrix for some large mixed-use developments can be very complex. However, as buildings become more sophisticated tenants can reasonably be expected to see this sophistication reflected in the method by which the service charge is apportioned in order to achieve (so far as is possible) reasonableness and fairness.

In all circumstances and whatever the basis used in calculating tenant apportionments of the service charge expenditure, an apportionment schedule should be made available to all occupiers showing the total apportionment for each unit within the property/complex.

Changing or altering apportionments

Fixed percentages

Where a tenant's service charge liability is stated as a fixed proportion the lease will usually allow for the landlord to vary the fixed percentage but only under certain circumstances, for example in the event that the building is altered or circumstances change so that the fixed percentage becomes unfair or unreasonable.

Where a commercial lease makes no provision for variation of the tenant's fixed percentage there is no obligation on the landlord to alter the tenant's contribution even if the result would be to allow the landlord to recover more than 100 per cent of the total expenditure. Nevertheless, if circumstances change to make the fixed percentage unfair or inequitable, the courts in certain circumstances may intervene and decide on an alternative fair method of apportioning the service charge.

As regards residential property, service charges are held in trust under section 42 of the LTA 1987. It therefore follows that while over 100 per cent can be collected in the above circumstances, it will be retained in the trust. It may, for example, be appropriate to pass the surplus to reserves thus reducing the required contribution to the reserve fund. In any event it will be necessary to comply with the accounting rules set out in chapter 5.

Fair and reasonable apportionment

Where a lease states that the tenants' proportion is to be calculated on a fair and reasonable basis, perhaps with reference to floor area, etc., the landlord would generally have the ability to alter a tenant's percentage apportionment from time to time in the event of any physical alteration to the building or to reflect some other change in circumstances.

9

Repairs, renewals, replacements and improvements

When granting a lease of premises forming part of a multi-occupied building a landlord will usually retain responsibility, amongst other things, for the maintenance and repair of the common areas, exterior and structure of the building. The tenant for its part will usually covenant to reimburse a proportion of the cost incurred by the landlord in complying with these retained obligations.

However, the subject of repairs has perhaps given rise to the largest number of reported cases regarding disputes in practice. This topic is a complex area of law and the context in which the word 'repair' appears in a particular lease, the nature of the defect involved and the extent or nature of remedial works proposed or required all have a significant bearing on matters and the weight attached to these matters will vary from case to case in determining the extent of the landlord's obligations to carry out works and the tenant's liability to contribute towards the costs incurred through the service charge. This chapter considers:

- Repairs, renewals and replacements
- Improvements
- Communication

9.1 Repairs, renewals and replacements

The precise wording of the lease may have a considerable impact upon the obligations of the respective parties to the lease with regard to repairs, renewals and replacements.

The distinction between repair and improvements is often very fine and it is not uncommon for less scrupulous landlords to seek to carry out refurbishment or improvement works under the pretext of repair and maintenance.

The law relating to repair is extensive and the wording of the definitions within the lease is crucially important; particularly in relation to repair and the definition of the demise and retained parts.

Generally speaking however, 'repair' has been defined as the rectifying of damage or deterioration or putting back into good condition something that, having been in good repair has fallen into bad condition.

Repair is the restoration by renewal or replacement of subsidiary parts of a whole. Renewal, as distinguished from repair, is reconstruction of the entirety, meaning not necessarily the whole but substantially the whole subject matter under discussion.

If the service charge provisions refer only to repair, then works that go beyond the scope of repair will fall outside the service charge. Unless expressly referred to, the landlord will generally be unable to recover the cost of improvements under the definition of repair.

9.2 Improvements

'If the work which is done is the provision of something new ... that is, properly speaking, an improvement; but if it is only the replacement of something already there, which has become dilapidated or worn out, then albeit that it is a replacement by its modern equivalent, it comes within the category of repairs and not improvements.' *(Denning LJ in Morcom v Campbell-Johnson [1955] 3 All ER 264)*

The distinction between repairs and improvements is often a question of degree and, in part, necessity. A landlord will usually have great difficulty in recovering the cost of improvements, as distinct from repairs, where this is not expressly covered in the lease.

9.3 Communication

While full and open communication with commercial tenants is considered essential for achieving best practice, practitioners should also be aware that it is not uncommon for commercial leases to set down clear conditions for the landlord to consult with tenants prior to incurring expenditure. Where such clear and unambiguous conditions exist, the need for consultation strictly in accordance with the requirements of the lease will usually be regarded as a condition precedent and failure to comply may leave the landlord unable to recover the expenditure incurred.

The following chapter deals with particular legislative requirements and rules for dealing with major works and improvements for residential property.

10

Major works and improvement rules

There are fundamental differences between the way in which these matters may be dealt with when managing commercial property or when dealing with residential leaseholders. A failure to follow the correct procedure is likely to result in an inability to recover the costs of the works involved from leaseholders. This is an area where the law overrides lease provisions. It is of paramount importance that you are fully aware of the rules if you are to be involved in residential leasehold management or advising lessees on their rights.

The current rules stem from the CLRA 2002 and are expanded by statutory instrument. They are considerably more complicated than those which applied under the LTA 1985 even though the legislation is an amendment to section 20 of the earlier Act. This chapter covers:

- What are major works and improvements?
- Do I need to serve a notice?
- How do I calculate the expenditure limits?
- The preliminary notice
- Replies to the preliminary notice
- Duty to have regard to observations received
- Preparing for the second notice
- The second notice
- Entering into the contract and do I need a third notice?
- Emergency works
- Right to apply to a Leasehold Valuation Tribunal to determine whether works are reasonable
- Need to include provisional cost sums
- Need to ensure that each schedule limit is known
- The effect on management costs

Statutory provision

Section 20 of the LTA 1985 as amended by the CLRA 2002 section 151 deals with major works and improvements. This inserts a new section 20 and 20ZA (SI 2003 No 1987).

10.1 What are major works and improvements?

The new section 20ZA defines qualifying works simply as 'works on a building or any other premises'. Under the revised section 20 'the relevant contributions of tenants' are limited unless the consultation requirements have been complied with or dispensed with by (or on appeal from) a Leasehold Valuation Tribunal.

The consultation limit for 'qualifying' works has been changed to a maximum contribution of £250 by any one or more payers. Whereas the previous limit was based on a flat sum per dwelling the new one is based upon the highest contribution payable by the tenant of any dwelling. In addition the lower limit of £1,000 has disappeared.

If there is more than one schedule to a building there is likely to be a different limit applying to each schedule and each must be worked out.

These figures need only be worked out again if the government changes the limit or the apportionment structure changes, BUT, as has already been mentioned, where there are different schedules different figures are likely to apply so take care.

It should also be noted that section 20 refers to the amount of relevant costs incurred in carrying out the works and SI 2003 No.1987 includes VAT where applicable. Clearly all costs to be incurred in the works must be included in the calculations if they are to be recovered.

10.2 Do I need to serve a notice?

This will depend upon whether or not the total cost of the proposed works including VAT and any associated professional fees or other expenses exceed the expenditure limits. If they do it will be necessary to issue notices. In practice it may well be necessary to obtain quotations in order to ascertain whether or not a notice is required. If the result indicates that notices are required it is good practice not to reveal the sums in the tenders until after the first notice has run its course and any further quotations are obtained.

There are two very good reasons for this. Firstly it would be unfair to the original tenderers if another firm could undercut them on the basis of their tender and secondly it is important that a contractor fully considers the work involved before quoting. If he or she does not, he or she may under price and then attempt to make up for this with shoddy work or inferior materials. If the works are extensive there is also a real risk of insolvency or a failure to complete.

10.3 How do I calculate the expenditure limits?

If the required contribution to the costs of the works of any one lessee exceeds £250 including VAT and any other associated costs or professional fees then notices are required.

This means that if a property is subject to more than one schedule with different apportionments then each schedule is likely to be the subject of a different limit. It is of paramount importance that these limits are calculated and known by the manager in order to avoid the potential for costly mistakes.

If everyone pays the same percentage the calculation is be fairly easy (£250 x no. flats).

If, on the other hand, we have a building which is multi-scheduled then we must take the highest apportionment in each schedule and use the formula:

Where a = the highest apportionment and m = the maximum payable before consultation (currently £250).

Examples

Example 1 – The highest apportionment is 3 per cent and the maximum amount is £250. The consultation will be for all figures above:	$\dfrac{1}{0.03} \times 250$	= £8,333.33
Example 2 – The largest apportionment is 75 per cent then the consultation will be for all sums above:	$\dfrac{1}{0.75} \times 250$	= £333.33

These figures need only be worked out again if the government changes the limit or the apportionment structure changes. BUT where there are different schedules different figures are likely to apply, so take care.

If the collection total is above 100 per cent the net apportionment should be used. The act deals with the actual contribution payable not a theoretical one.

10.4 The preliminary notice

In cases where a public notice is not required under European Union rules, this is described in SI 2003 No. 1987 paragraph 35 as a 'Notice of intention' (public consultation requirements are not dealt with within the scope of this book).

There is no prescribed form to this notice but there are statutory requirements as to what it must contain and who it must be sent to. Care should be taken to comply with these requirements and to avoid material within the notice which may be interpreted as invalidating it. Lessees for example are invited to make observations in relation to the proposed works. It can therefore be argued that if a specification is provided it should include any conditions required of contractors. The inclusion of unequivocal conditions on the face of the notice which are then found to have been unreasonable might invalidate the notice whereas if they form part of the specification the lessees have the right to comment on them and make their point. A response by the landlord can then be made in the second notice.

The landlord shall give notice **in writing** of his or her intention to carry out qualifying works:

- to each tenant; **and**
- to a recognised residents association representing any or all of the tenants.

The notice shall:

- describe, in general terms, the works to be carried out or specify the place and hours at which a description of the proposed works may be inspected;
- state the Landlords reasons for considering it necessary to carry out the proposed works;
- invite the making in writing of observations in relation to the proposed works
- specify the address to which such observations may be sent and that they must be delivered within the relevant period (30 days); and
- state the date on which the relevant period ends.

The notice shall also invite each tenant and association (if any) to propose within the relevant period, the name of a person from whom the landlord should try to obtain an estimate for carrying out the proposed works.

Where the notice specifies a place and hours for inspection:

- the place and hours so specified must be reasonable; and
- the description of the proposed works must be available for inspection, free of charge, at that place and during those hours.

If copying facilities are not available at the above, a copy of the description must be provided by the landlord on request and free of charge.

The landlord has a duty to have regard to observations made during the relevant period.

The landlord must try to obtain an estimate from the nominated person if made by the residents association regardless of whether or not a nomination is made by the tenants.

He or she must also try to obtain one from any single nomination of a tenant if there is only one.

If there is more than one tenant nomination then the landlord must obtain an estimate from the one with the most nominations.

In practice if the specification is reasonably short it is worth sending one with each notice, which will then avoid the need to provide for inspection. Where there are on-site office facilities and staff provision could be made for tenants to collect a copy if they wanted one. In practice demand would vary from block to block but the papers would be seen to be readily and easily available to anyone who wanted a copy.

10.5 Replies to the preliminary notice

It is very important to note that this is the tenant's opportunity to:

- a. propose contractors from whom landlords are obliged to seek quotations; and
- b. make written observations regarding the proposed works.

These rights must be exercised in writing and within the consultation period.

As the consultation procedure is somewhat convoluted, tenants and those advising them should appreciate that if they wish to propose a contractor this is the time to do it and not at a later stage when they do not like the result of the subsequent tender. After this stage is finished there is no further right to propose contractors.

From the manager's point of view it may well be helpful to draw this fact to the attention of the tenants when issuing the preliminary notice.

10.6 Duty to have regard to observations received

Where within the time period observations are made in relation to the proposed works by any tenant or recognised residents association, the landlord shall have regard to those observations. This obligation is quite plain and cannot be avoided.

The landlord must try to obtain an estimate from the nominated person if made by the residents association regardless of whether or not a nomination is made by the tenants. He or she must **also** try to obtain one from any single nomination of a tenant if there is only one. If there is more than one tenant nomination then the landlord must obtain an estimate from the one with the most nominations.

10.7 Preparing for the second notice

When the preliminary notice has run its course the Landlord **must** try to obtain an estimate from the nominated person if made by the residents association regardless of whether or not a nomination is made by the tenants. He or she must **also** try to obtain one from any single nomination of a resident if there is only one.

If there is more than one tenant nomination then the landlord must obtain an estimate from the one with the most nominations.

You may come to the conclusion that despite the rules, within reason, all recommended contractors who come up to an acceptable standard should be invited to tender. It appears that even if they do not it may still be necessary to attempt to obtain a tender from them if they come within the category of those from whom tenders should be obtained. The system provides for giving reasons for not appointing contractors at a later stage.

It should also be noted that nothing stops you from sending out tender documents or requests for quotations during the preliminary notice period as recommendations are received but it may be necessary to vary the specification in the light of observations received later during the period. This is an area in which urgency, scope, complication, and many other factors will need to be assessed in order to determine the appropriate course of action.

In any event you will need to obtain tenders from at least two contractors and while these can both be from tenant nominations, you will need to make your own choices if they are not forthcoming.

Consideration should be given to the need or otherwise to provide provisional cost sums within the notice and specifications to provide for extra works which may become evident during the course of the works.

10.8 The second notice

Having obtained the estimates the landlord must supply free of charge a statement setting out:

- the amount specified in at least two of the estimates as the estimated cost of the proposed works;
- where the landlord has received observations to which he or she is required to have regard a summary of the observations and his or her response to them;
- the estimates must be made available for inspection;
- at least one of the estimates must be from a person wholly unconnected with the landlord (see paragraph 38 (7) SI 2003 No. 1987 for a definition of connected persons); and
- if an estimate has been obtained from a nominated person, from whom the landlord is obliged to seek one, the landlord must include that estimate in the statement.

The statement must be supplied to all tenants and any recognised residents associations. It must include a copy of the estimates or specify:

- the place and hours at which the estimates may be inspected;
- invite the making in writing of observations in relation to the estimates;
- specify the address to which such observations may be sent and that they must be delivered within the relevant period. (30 days); and
- state the date on which the relevant period ends.

If copying facilities are not available at the place at which the estimates may be inspected a copy of the estimates must be provided by the landlord on request and free of charge.

In practice it may well be easier to supply copies with the notice if they are not extensive.

Where within the time period observations are made in relation to the estimates by any tenant or recognised residents association, the landlord shall have regard to those observations. Again this obligation is quite plain and cannot be avoided.

The notice should include VAT and any other costs involved (e.g. professional fees and provisional cost sums).

10.9 Entering into the contract and do I need a third notice?

Finally within 21 days of entering into a contract the landlord shall by notice in writing to each tenant and secretary of any recognised residents association:

- state his or her reasons for awarding the contract or a place and time at which they can be inspected. (If copying facilities are not available at the place mentioned a copy of the estimates must be provided by the landlord on request and free of charge.); and
- where he or she has received observations to which he or she is required to have regard, a summary of those observations and the response to them.

Unless the person to whom the contract was awarded was a nominated person or submitted the lowest estimate.

Be careful with the definition of nominated person. If you have included a tenant nomination in addition to the one with the most nominations he or she may not be a nominated person for the purposes of this section!

It is somewhat interesting to note that a third notice is not required even if the nominated contractor is far more expensive than the rest, but is required if a contractor is awarded the contract who is marginally more expensive than the cheapest but far cheaper than a nominated contractor! You must also bear in mind the right to challenge any decision at the Leasehold Valuation Tribunal.

10.10 Emergency works

Under the old system a single notice was required and works could not begin until after it had run its course or to quote the Act: 'unless the works are urgently required'. ***This wording has been removed from the new legislation.***

It follows that if works are 'qualifying works' then to be sure of recovering the costs even in an emergency situation, it will be necessary to make an application to the Leasehold Valuation Tribunal to dispense with the consultation requirements.

It appears that this is also the case where extra works come to light during an ongoing project.

Given that the maximum possible amount at which the notice procedure comes into force when a conversion to two flats is involved must be no more than £500 (two flats paying 50 per cent each), it is not difficult to see that the need for such an application is likely to occur frequently for this type of property. If one flat pays more than 50 per cent then the threshold will be even lower.

The Residential Property Tribunal Service has made provision for Leasehold Valuation Tribunals to hear emergency applications in these circumstances but one has to observe that the costs involved particularly to leaseholders may outweigh any potential benefits where the sums are less than the previous cut off of £1,000.

10.11 Right to apply to a Leasehold Valuation Tribunal to determine whether works are reasonable

In cases where doubts arise as to the reasonableness of proposed works it is open both to the Landlord and tenants to make an application to the LVT to determine whether or what works are reasonable and whether or not proposed costs are reasonable before the work commences.

If there is any doubt from the landlord's point of view or he or she has reason to believe that costs will be challenged then he or she should seriously consider making an application as this will prevent a challenge after costs have been incurred.

From the tenant's point of view an application at an early stage may clarify matters. The scope of works can also be considered and the relative long-term advantages dealt with.

It is important for both sides to note that the Leasehold Valuation Tribunal will have to work within the statutory rules and will look towards the building being reasonably maintained at a reasonable cost. It will also have to bear in mind the costs of contractors and landlords complying with legislation. It is not unknown for a small building contractor to be blissfully unaware of what CDM (*Construction (Design and Management) Regulations* 2007) means let alone complying with it! This provides an excellent reason for not contracting the services but in fairness to the tenant he or she may not understand why.

10.12 Need to include provisional cost sums

Now that the consultation procedure has become much more truncated the need to provide reasonable provisional cost sums to allow for unquantified extra work is even more important than it was.

In *Martin and another v Maryland Estates Ltd* CA [1999] 26 EG 151 it was established that extra works which came to light during a programme required a further notice and that as they were executed as an additional part of the original programme it was necessary to issue a new notice for **any works** which exceeded the original notice costs.

The judge's reasoning was that this would make the lessees aware of the proposed extra costs at the time rather than when the bill arrived up to eighteen months later. Quite how this fits in with the new two notice system remains to be seen as the old legislation allowed a start in an emergency before the notice had run out. It may well be that under the new rules an emergency application to the Leasehold Valuation Tribunal is the appropriate course of action.

It is however clear that if this can be avoided it will generally be desirable all round.

When dealing with provisional cost sums in the second notice it may be necessary to make some adjustments so that the tenders can be compared on a like for like basis.

It may also be necessary to require schedules of rates to apply to these. It is sometimes useful to ask contractors to suggest appropriate provisional cost sums. If you do this you are likely to need to adjust so that the quotations can be compared on a like for like basis. You could also provide set provisional cost sums within the specification and require the contractors to state if they feel that these are inadequate.

10.13 Need to ensure that each schedule limit is known

If the required contribution to the works of any one lessee exceeds £250 then notices are required.

The new regime is far more complicated than the original one and in some cases the limits have actually reduced. There is now no set minimum nor is the figure calculated by dividing the total costs by the number of flats as before.

This means that if a property is subject to more than one schedule with different apportionments then each schedule is likely to be the subject of a different limit. It is of paramount importance that these limits are calculated and known by the manager in order to avoid the potential for costly mistakes.

If everyone pays the same percentage the calculation is fairly easy (£250 x no of flats).

If, on the other hand, we have a building which is multi-scheduled then we must take the highest apportionment in each schedule and use the formula:

$$\frac{l}{a} \times m$$

Where a = the highest apportionment and m = the maximum payable before consultation (currently £250).

Example

A block of ten flats has three schedules

Schedule A Car Park – each flat 10 per cent

All apportionments are 10 per cent and the maximum amount is £250 the consultation will be for all figures above:

$$\frac{1}{0.1} \times 250 = £2500.00$$

Schedule B General Maintenance – all contribute but highest apportionment 12.5 per cent

The highest apportionment is 12.5 per cent and the maximum amount is £250 the consultation will be for all figures above:

$$\frac{1}{0.125} \times 250 = £2000.00$$

Schedule C Lift – only five flats contribute highest apportionment 24 per cent

The highest apportionment is 24 per cent and the maximum amount is £250 the consultation will be for all figures above:

$$\frac{1}{0.24} \times 250 = £1041.67$$

As can be seen there is a wide range of limits and the lower one is less than half that of the higher. In the lower case of course it is only necessary to serve the notice on the five contributing tenants.

10.14 The effect on management costs

The effect on management costs can be considerable particularly when the works involved only affect a small number of flats. Parliament has however decided that the consultation should take place and until the rules are changed we all have to live with them. We must ensure that costs of consultation charged back to the tenants are reasonable but this must be in-line with the work which is required.

Where large numbers of flats are involved the limits have increased by up to five-fold but the removal of the £1,000 minimum has seen a large increase in the amount of work covered where only a few flats are concerned. It is of particular concern where an owner occupier owns the freehold of a small block in which he or she lives. In many of these cases professional management will be relatively costly and the potential for the honest and diligent freeholder to lose out through ignorance is a matter for concern.

11

Dealing with long-term agreements

The CLRA 2002 has extended the consultation process for residential leasehold property to cover long-term agreements. This means that it will no longer be possible to sign-up a long-term leasing or other contract without a consultation.

- What are not long-term agreements?
- What are qualifying long-term agreements?
- Do I need to serve a notice?
- How do I calculate the expenditure limit?
- The preliminary notice or notice of intention
- Replies to the preliminary notice
- Duty to have regard to observations received
- Preparing for the second notice
- The second notice
- Entering into the contract and do I need a third notice?
- Right to apply to a Leasehold Valuation Tribunal to determine whether it is reasonable to enter into an agreement
- Need to ensure that each schedule limit is known
- The effect on management costs

Statutory provision

Section 20 LTA 1985 as amended by CLRA 2002 section 151 deals with long-term agreements. This inserts a new section 20 and 20ZA (*The Service Charges (Consultation Requirements) (England) Regulations*, SI 2003/1987).

11.1 What are not long-term agreements?

The following are NOT long-term agreements:

- contracts of employment;
- if it is a management agreement made by a Local Housing Authority and a Tenant Management Organisation or a body established under section 2 of the *Local Government Act* 2000;
- contracts between holding companies and subsidiaries or between their subsidiaries;
- if when the agreement was entered into there are no tenants of the building or other premises to which the agreement relates and the agreement does not exceed five years; and
- if it was entered into before the effective date in October 2003 when the regulations came into force.

11.2 What are qualifying long-term agreements?

Qualifying agreements are those entered into for a period of more than twelve months where any lessee will be liable to pay more than £100 in any accounting period.

It may be that the use of accounting periods, as opposed to actual years may produce interesting results and I suggest that you consider this. The requirement relates to agreements of more than one year but not to those which can be brought to an end within that period (e.g. a management contract with a six months notice period or any other rolling contract which can be brought to an end within a year). It will cover for example leasing arrangements for security systems, television aerials and satellite systems, door entry systems and long-term servicing arrangements together with energy management systems and any other arrangement which involves expenditure over the qualifying limit. Take care with insurance!

The authors have their own views on leasing arrangements particularly when lessors seek to lease equipment that should properly have been included as part of the original design and development specification.

This can often be seen as a way of passing costs onto the service charge that ought properly have formed part of the developer's capital cost.

Where a decision is taken to lease new equipment, there is often a risk that the standard of maintenance and repair would be at the behest of the leasing company. Problems can therefore arise if the service provider allows their systems to deteriorate, which leads to an increase in expenditure to bring them back to a reasonable standard. However at the end of the day the new procedure does not outlaw such leasing arrangements, but it does require consultation with tenants.

11.3 Do I need to serve a notice?

This will depend upon whether or not the total costs of the proposed agreement including VAT exceed the expenditure limits. If they do it will be necessary to issue notices. In practice it may well be necessary to obtain quotations in order to ascertain whether or not a notice is required. If the result indicates that notices are required it is good practice not to reveal the sums in the tenders until after the first notice has run its course and any further quotations are obtained.

There are two very good reasons for this: firstly it would be unfair to the original tenderers if another firm could undercut them on the basis of their tender; and secondly it is important that a contractor fully considers the work involved before quoting. If he or she does not, he or she may under price and then attempt to make up for this with shoddy work or inferior materials.

11.4 How do I calculate the expenditure limits?

If the required contribution in any accounting period to the costs of the agreement of any one lessee exceeds £100 including VAT and any other costs then notices are required.

This means that if a property is subject to more than one schedule with different apportionments then each schedule is likely to be the subject of a different limit. It is of paramount importance that these limits are calculated and known by the manager in order to avoid the potential for costly mistakes.

If everyone pays the same percentage the calculation is fairly easy (**£100 x no. of flats**).

If, on the other hand, there is a building which is multi-scheduled then you must take the highest apportionment in each schedule and use the formula:

$$\frac{1}{a} \times m$$

Where a = the highest apportionment and m = the maximum payable before consultation (currently £100).

Examples

Example 1 – The highest apportionment is 3 per cent and the maximum amount is £100 the consultation will be for all figures above:	$\frac{1}{0.03} \times 100$	= £3,333.33
Example 2 – The largest apportionment is 75 per cent then the consultation will be for all sums above:	$\frac{1}{0.75} \times 100$	= £133.33

These figures need only be worked out again if the government changes the limit or the apportionment structure changes, BUT as I have already said where there are different schedules different figures are likely to apply so care will need to be taken.

If the collection total is above 100 per cent the net apportionment should be used. The act deals with the actual contribution payable not a theoretical one.

If the proposed agreement contains a clause which may apply increases to bring the contributions above the limit during its life, then a consultation should be held or a cap included to prevent this.

11.5 The preliminary notice or notice of intention

In cases where a public notice is not required under European Union rules, this is described in SI 2003 No. 1987 paragraph 8 as a 'Notice of intention' (public consultation requirements are not dealt with within then scope of this book).

There is no prescribed form to this notice but there are statutory requirements as to what it must contain and who it must be sent to. Care should be taken to comply with these requirements and to avoid material within the notice which may be interpreted as invalidating it. Lessees for example are invited to comment on relevant matters. It can therefore be argued that this is the place in which to specify any conditions required of contractors. The inclusion of unequivocal conditions on the face of the notice which are then found to have been unreasonable might invalidate the notice whereas if they form part of the relevant matters section the lessees have the right to comment on them and make their point. A response can then be made in the second notice.

The landlord shall give notice **in writing** of his or her intention to enter into the agreement:

- to each tenant; **and**
- to a recognised residents association representing any or all of the tenants.

The notice shall:

- describe, in general terms, the relevant matters or specify the place and hours at which a description of the relevant matters may be inspected;
- state the landlord's reasons for considering it necessary to enter into the agreement;
- where the relevant matters consist of or include qualifying works, state the landlord's reasons for considering it necessary to carry out those works;
- invite the making in writing of observations in relation to the proposed agreement;
- specify the address to which such observations may be sent and that they must be delivered within the relevant period (30 days); and
- state the date on which the relevant period ends.

The notice shall also invite each tenant and association (if any) to propose within the relevant period, the name of a person from whom the landlord should try to obtain an estimate for the relevant matters.

Where the notice specifies a place and hours for inspection:

- the place and hours so specified must be reasonable; and
- the description of the relevant matters must be available for inspection, free of charge, at that place and during those hours.

If copying facilities are not available at the above premises, a copy must be provided by the landlord on request and free of charge.

The landlord has a duty to have regard to observations made during the relevant period.

The landlord must try to obtain an estimate from the nominated person if made by the residents association regardless of whether or not a nomination is made by the tenants. He or she must **also** try to obtain one from any single nomination of a resident if there is only one.

If there is more than one tenant nomination then the landlord must obtain an estimate from the one with the most nominations.

11.6 Replies to the preliminary notice

It is very important to note that this is the tenant's opportunity to:

- propose contractors from whom landlords are obliged to seek quotations; and
- make written observations regarding the relevant matters.

These rights must be exercised in writing and within the consultation period.

As the consultation procedure is somewhat truncated, tenants and those advising them should appreciate that if they wish to propose a contractor this is the time to do it and not at a later stage if they do not like the result of the subsequent tender. After this stage is finished there is no further right to propose contractors.

From the managers point of view it may well be helpful to draw this fact to the attention of the tenants when issuing the preliminary notice.

11.7 Duty to have regard to observations received

Where within the time period observations are made in relation to the relevant matters by any tenant or recognised residents association, the landlord shall have regard to those observations. This obligation is quite plain and cannot be avoided.

The landlord must try to obtain an estimate from the nominated person if made by the residents association regardless of whether or not a nomination is made by the tenants. He or she must **also** try to obtain one from any single nomination of a resident if there is only one.

If there is more than one tenant nomination then the landlord must obtain an estimate from the one with the most nominations.

11.8 Preparing for the second notice

When the preliminary notice has run its course the Landlord must try to obtain an estimate from the nominated person if made by the residents association regardless of whether or not a nomination is made by the tenants. He or she must **also** try to obtain one from any single nomination of a resident if there is only one.

If there is more than one tenant nomination then the landlord must obtain an estimate from the one with the most nominations.

You may come to the conclusion that despite the rules, within reason, all recommended contractors who come up to an acceptable standard should be invited to tender. It appears that even if they do not it may still be necessary to attempt to obtain a tender from them if they come within the category of those from whom tenders should be obtained. The system provides for giving reasons for not appointing contractors at a later stage.

It should also be noted that nothing stops you from sending out tender documents or requests for quotations during the preliminary notice period as recommendations are received but it may be necessary to vary the specification in the light of observations received later during the period. This is an area in which urgency, scope, complication, and many other factors will need to be assessed in order to determine the appropriate course of action.

11.9 The second notice

Having obtained the estimates the landlord must prepare at least two proposals in respect of the relevant matters:

- at least one of the proposals must be from a person wholly unconnected with the landlord (see paragraph 38 (7) SI 2003 No. 1987 for a definition of connected persons);
- if an estimate has been obtained from a nominated person, from whom the landlord is obliged to seek one, the landlord must prepare a proposal based on that estimate;
- each proposal must contain a statement of the relevant matters; and
- each proposal must contain a statement, as regards each party to the proposed agreement other than the landlord:
- of the parties name and address; and
- of any connection (apart from the proposed agreement) between the party and the landlord (see paragraph. 12 (6) SI 2003 No. 1987 for a definition of connection).

Where reasonable to do so the statement should include the relevant contribution attributable to each tenant. If this is not reasonably practicable then an estimate of the costs for the entire building will suffice. If this is not practicable then unit costs hourly or daily rates should be included if possible.

If the contract refers to the appointment of an agent to carry out any of the landlord's duties in relation to the management of the property then the proposal shall contain a statement:

That the person whose appointment is proposed:

(a) is or is not a member of a professional body or trade association;

(b) does or does not subscribe to any code of practice or voluntary accreditation scheme relevant to the functions of managing agents; and

(c) if the person is a member of a professional body or trade association the name of the body or association.

Each proposal shall contain a statement as to the provisions (if any) for the variation of any amount specified or to be determined under the proposed agreement.

Each proposal shall contain a statement of the intended duration of the agreement.

Where observations have been received that the landlord is obliged to have regard to, each proposal must contain a summary of those observations and the landlord's response.

Notice in writing of the proposals must be given to all tenants and any recognised residents associations, which must include a copy of the proposals or specify:

(a) the place and hours at which the proposals may be inspected;
(b) invite the making in writing of observations in relation to the proposals;
(c) specify the address to which such observations may be sent and that they must be delivered within the relevant period. (30 days); and
(d) state the date on which the relevant period ends.

If copying facilities are not available at the above a copy of the estimates must be provided by the landlord on request and free of charge.

In practice it may well be easier to supply copies with the notice if they are not extensive.

Where within the time period observations are made in relation to the proposals by any tenant or recognised residents association, the landlord shall have regard to those observations. Again this obligation is quite plain and cannot be avoided.

The notice should include VAT and any other costs involved.

11.10 Entering into the contract and do I need a third notice?

According to the *Service Charges (Consultation Requirements) (England) Regulations* 2003 within 21 days of entering into a contract the landlord shall by notice in writing to each tenant and secretary of any recognised residents association:

(a)   state his or her reasons for entering into the contract or a place and time at which they can be inspected. (If copying facilities are not available at the above a copy of the estimates must be provided by the landlord on request and free of charge.); and

(b)   where he or she has received observations to which he or she is required to have regard, a summary of those observations and his or her response to them.

Unless the person to whom the contract was awarded was a nominated person or submitted the lowest estimate.

Be careful with the definition of nominated person.

It is somewhat interesting to note that a third notice is not required even if the nominated contractor is far more expensive than the rest, but is required if a contractor who is marginally more expensive than the cheapest but far cheaper than a nominated contractor is awarded the contract. You must also bear in mind the right to challenge any decision at the Leasehold Valuation Tribunal.

11.11 Right to apply to a Leasehold Valuation Tribunal to determine whether it is reasonable to enter into an agreement

In cases where doubts arise as to the reasonableness of proposed works it is open both to the landlord and tenants to make an application to the Leasehold Valuation Tribunal to determine whether or what works are reasonable and whether or not proposed costs are reasonable before the agreement commences.

If there is any doubt from the landlord's point of view or he or she has reason to believe that costs will be challenged then he or she should seriously consider making an application as this will prevent a challenge after a binding contract has been entered into.

From the tenant's point of view an application at an early stage may clarify matters.

It is important for both sides to note that the Leasehold Valuation Tribunal will have to work within the statutory rules and will look towards the building being reasonably maintained at a reasonable cost. It will also have to bear in mind the costs of contractors and landlords complying with legislation. It may however consider that these interests may not be best served by a long-term agreement.

11.12 Need to ensure that each schedule limit is known

If the required contribution, to a qualifying long-term agreement, of any one lessee exceeds £100 in any accounting period then notices are required.

This means that if a property is subject to more than one schedule with different apportionments then each schedule is likely to be the subject of a different overall limit. It is of paramount importance that these limits are calculated and known by the manager in order to avoid the potential for costly mistakes.

If everyone pays the same percentage the calculation is fairly easy (£100 x no of flats). If on the other hand we have a building which is multi-scheduled then we must take the highest apportionment in each schedule and use the formula:

$$\frac{1}{a} \times m$$

Where a = the highest apportionment and m = the maximum payable before consultation (currently £100).

Example

A block of 20 flats has three schedules

Schedule A Gardens – each flat pays 5 per cent

All apportionments are 5 per cent and the maximum amount is £100 the consultation will be for all figures above:

$$\frac{1}{0.05} \times 100 = £2000.00$$

Schedule B General Maintenance – all contribute but highest apportionment 9 per cent

The highest apportionment is 9 per cent and the maximum amount is £100 the consultation will be for all figures above:

$$\frac{1}{0.09} \times 100 = £1111.11$$

Schedule C Lift – 10 flats contribute highest apportionment 13 per cent

The highest apportionment is 13 per cent and the maximum amount is £100 the consultation will be for all figures above:

$$\frac{1}{0.13} \times 100 = £884.96$$

As can be seen differing apportionments can have a significant effect on the level of contract figure that requires consultation. In reality consultations will often be needed on relatively low value contracts or in cases where figures are well within the norm for a particular service.

11.13 The effect on management costs

There is a significant difference between a long-term agreement and major works in that in most cases the need to enter into a long-term agreement is not a necessity and there is usually an alternative.

Long-term agreements are popular with some developers in that they transfer capital costs for equipment to lessees (e.g. satellite and TV aerials and door entry systems). They also enable them to appoint managers and agree other contracts on which they may receive commissions. To an extent this continues but the contracts are limited to five years and must be entered into before any of the flats in a building are sold.

On the other hand lessees may prefer to enter into a rental system in order to avoid significant capital expenditure especially if a significant number are having difficulty meeting service charge demands. The new system simply ensures that this can only be done following a set consultation process.

The new right to manage provisions may well have a marked effect on the willingness of contractors to provide rental services in any event but that is a subject to be dealt with elsewhere and will no doubt evolve. Potential liabilities in the event of the right being exercised, should however be considered.

Clearly the new provisions will significantly increase the management costs of entering into a long-term agreement and are likely to make these less common as a result. This is probably no bad thing overall. If there is a clear advantage to a long-term agreement then the consultation will be worthwhile.

12

Year-end accounts

A service charge will often provide for the service costs incurred by the landlord to be certified by the landlord's surveyor or accountant. Where statutory regulation imposes obligations upon a landlord of residential property this is usually to be viewed as being in addition to and not instead of any specific requirements or obligations set down in the lease – so far as the lease terms are not inconsistent with the statute. This chapter considers:

- Pulling everything together
- Schedules
- Accruals and prepayments
- Transfers to reserves at year-end
- Form of accounts
- Certification – What is it? Final and binding
- What does 'save as to manifest error mean'?
- Rights to inspect documents
- External audit of accounts – need to ensure accountant is familiar with this type of work

The preparation of the year-end accounts should not be seen solely as a chore to be completed as quickly as possible but as an opportunity to review the management of the property and check that everything is running smoothly. Ideally the accounts submitted by you to the accountants should not require any alteration.

If you are able to produce consistent and accurate final accounts there will be two distinct advantages: firstly accountancy fees payable by your clients (and often recovered from tenants through the service charge) should be lower; and secondly your time and that of the accountant should not be wasted dealing with long lists of queries and confirmations brought about by errors and inaccuracies.

Modern property management systems allow the production of accounts which are scheduled and balanced but they cannot (completely at least) correct errors in inputs and miss-postings to incorrect schedules. It may be that some invoices need splitting between several schedules and others require detailed attention as to exactly where they should be posted. In these complicated cases it may be appropriate to take a deliberate decision to review certain schedules at the year-end. If you have taken this course you will then need to follow it through.

Whatever systems you may have in place to prevent contractor overcharging and double invoicing, the year-end provides an opportunity to check that this is not happening. Utility bills are particularly susceptible to double payment as these accounts rarely use invoice numbers, are often 'reissued' seemingly for no reason for a different amount, and arrive at unpredictable times demanding prompt settlement.

Although one may be able to remember receiving a contractor's bill before authorising it and the system may be set up to reject duplicates; remembering every utility bill or setting your system to reject them is either more complicated than it is worth or very expensive.

There is also a need to consider that 'accidental' rejection of payments of utility accounts can lead to very unfortunate circumstances such as disconnection and as a result prompt payment requirements may sometimes override the systems which are in place for meticulous checking prior to settlement.

There are differing views on the merits of the right to inspect accounts but on serious reflection it is not hard to conclude that neatly prepared invoices which can be traced directly to the print outs should instil confidence on the part of the lessees that things have indeed been run efficiently.

12.1 Pulling everything together

Initially the accounts department will need to print off the schedules and produce the purchase invoices in the order of its printed schedule. These should be vouched to ensure that they are all there and correctly entered.

A review should then be carried out to ensure that all invoices are posted to the correct schedule and, if applicable, heading within that schedule. It will depend upon your organisation exactly who does this but it is probably as much a management function as an accounting one. Whoever is setting the budget should understand this area of the work.

The manager may also be able to identify any obvious errors omissions or miss-postings. At the same time a review of the year's accounts may serve to remind him or her of something which needs attention or to consider other matters (e.g. value for money and the relevance of continuing services).

There will of course always be time and cost limitations but experience over the years leads the authors to the conclusion that the experienced property manager reviewing the accounts at this stage is highly desirable. Many things can be revealed which will lead to better overall management. Individual repair invoices spread over a year may point to the need for major works or the incompetence of a contractor. Items which should have been included in contracts may have been charged for. Unauthorised price increases may have crept in. The list is almost endless.

Such a review can of course be carried out at any stage but it is more cost effective to combine it with the needs of the year-end accounts. It will also highlight any major changes which have occurred since the budget was set.

You will need to ensure that invoices arriving close to the year-end are included in it. Generally when the invoices are regular it is easy to see when they have crept into the next year. In many cases the actual invoice date will need to be altered for posting purposes where the property management system uses invoice dates to prepare its accounts. While trading companies running on net monthly accounts will tend to put the appropriate dates on their invoices to avoid settlement a month later, small tradesmen and utility companies seem to expect payment within days of issuing their invoice. Unfortunately this expectation leads to less care being used to ensure that their invoice date is the actual supply date.

12.2 Schedules

Schedules are used where different apportionments apply to different lessees at different rates – in other words where liability differs from a single standard fraction of all expenditure to each lessee. This matter is dealt with elsewhere in this work but it is imperative that all expenditure has been placed into the correct schedule when the year-end accounts are produced. You cannot simply roll forward a pot of surplus money to the next year on a multi-scheduled building without creating major problems. This should be obvious but I have seen a situation where it has occurred over a number of years – calculating who owed and was owed exactly how much was an extremely time consuming exercise.

The reason why a roll-on should not occur is that each schedule belongs to each lessee in different proportions and the money must stay in its schedule. If you wish to retain funds then they should be transferred to reserves for the individual schedules which are in surplus.

Under the residential rules where money cannot be recovered more than 18 months after expenditure is incurred unless notice is given, there is a potential serious problem if some lessees are actually in deficit.

12.3 Accruals and prepayments

When you have put everything together into its schedule you need to deal with accruals and prepayments. As discussed elsewhere prepayments are best avoided as they lead to cash flow problems and do not reflect actual service charge expenditure which is what you need to recover. Accruals on the other hand are required to give a true picture of the expenditure incurred for the period which needs to be recovered.

In the main accruals will need to be made for accountancy and audit fees relating to the period, and any other charges for it which have not been invoiced and included. These may include some management fees if paid in arrears, costs of works carried out but not invoiced and any other expenses relating to the period which have not been invoiced but nevertheless applied to it. In effect there are many possibilities not least from some tradesmen who can never get their bills in on time!

TIP

As many property management systems function on invoice date, provision for accruals will create a problem as the invoice is not to hand. In order to get the system to work, create a separate 'fund' (e.g. 'service charge brought forward'). Transfer at year-end date a separate sum from each schedule as appropriate to cover accruals into this fund.

This fund can also be used to charge back items to lessees that may not be recoverable. These items are rare but as residential service charges cannot be recovered more than 18 months after they were incurred it is not desirable to present accounts showing recoveries which have not been made and may be written off. Interest on late payments and charges for repairs direct to lessees are examples of charges which may on consideration be written-off at a later date in the light of explanations received.

Monies held in this fund can then be settled against the accrued invoices when they are received during the next service charge period without adversely affecting the way in which the property management system calculates the next year's accounts.

If uncertain monies are recovered or the accruals were over provided these monies can be transferred back into the main fund during the next year. They can then show as credits for the next period.

A separate print out for this fund can of course be supplied to the accountants to verify matters. Reconciliation of this fund will of course form part of the year-end accounting procedure.

12.4 Transfers to reserves at year-end

A landlord is only entitled to apply monies to a reserve fund which are fair and reasonable. This may mean that commercial property is treated in a very different way to residential, not least because of the term of the leases involved and the ultimate beneficiary of the fund. The terms of the lease setting up the reserve fund will have to be adhered to, in so far as they do not conflict with statute. If the lease sets out conditions for assessing or certifying the fund they must be followed.

In *St Mary's Mansions Ltd v Limegate Investments Co. Ltd* the reserve fund was certified by an accountant and the landlord then attempted to transfer the year-end surplus in addition to the certified requirement to the reserve fund. The court held that:

> A landlord is only entitled to apply monies to a reserve fund which are fair and reasonable and in respect of

133

specifically identified expenditure for which the reserve fund was created rather than other, unidentified, future expenses. A landlord cannot arbitrarily transfer a surplus in the on-account service charge payments made by tenants to a reserve fund.

If you wish to retain any surplus for the year then this should be taken as a transfer to each schedule reserve fund at the year-end. The sum transferred should be equal to the remaining surplus in each schedule once everything else including all accruals has been charged. This would be subject to the terms of the lease and it is good practice in any event to indicate that you intend to do this in the original budget.

If the accounts are to be the subject of an audit or certification you will need to make it clear to the accountant that if his or her fee differs from your accrual then a corresponding adjustment will need to be made as appropriate to whichever schedule or schedules his or her fees are charged. Likewise if there are to be any alterations anywhere else a similar adjustment will have to be made.

It is of paramount importance that the accountant's figures tie in with your property management system and that any adjustments as appropriate are made to it and any errors in his or her figures are agreed and corrected!

You should not finalise your system for a year until the accountant has produced his or her accounts. Once this has been done your property management system should be able to demand any balancing charges or as appropriate award credits.

12.5 Form of accounts

Form of accounts are discussed in chapter 5. Residential properties need to comply with the requirements of section 21 of the LTA 1985 as amended. Commercial properties benefit from complying with the code to good practice.

In any event the accounts should be clear and deal with individual schedules in such a way that they can be distinguished and the monies within each reconciled by the contributors.

Residential properties are covered by section 42 of the LTA 1987 which means that the funds **are not the funds of the management company or landlord**. They are held on trust. Accountants who are tempted to place these funds within the assets of any management company should have regard to the provisions of the *Companies Act* to show a true and fair picture of the state of the company. It is difficult to see how this can possibly be done if money held on trust is shown as an asset of the company or landlord.

It is often said that as the management company belongs to the lessees it makes no difference. That is not an opinion to which the authors subscribe in any case but if the management company is owned equally and the service charge payable by different proportions it clearly makes a considerable difference!

It is also not uncommon for a lessee-owned company to acquire the freehold of a residential building and yet shares in it remain with owners when they subsequently sell their leases.

The management company may well have other assets and liabilities and it is important to ring-fence the service charge funds from these.

In addition to the standard accounts the requirements of leases may impose a need to supply additional information. Your property management system may well be able to provide this in the form of a report.

12.6 Certification – what is it? Final and binding

The form of certificate required for commercial property will depend upon the lease terms and may well be one from the managing agents.

Residential service charges fall within section 21 of the LTA 1985 as amended. It is sometimes amusing listening to members of the accountancy profession discussing what they are willing to provide and the finer points of audit or certification. At the end of the day the requirement is in the statute. To be fair residential service charges are probably the only area in which many accountants are likely to practice where the contract (lease) is so heavily over ridden by statute. In the residential sector most practising chartered surveyors on the other hand have never seen a time where statutory intervention has not been draconian in some part of our work.

In the commercial sector strict time limits have been rare but the Code of Practice for *Service Charges in Commercial Property* sets out to change this position drastically.

The residential sector is moving towards compulsory certification within six months of the year-end. In some cases (possibly all in the future), a failure to comply will be a criminal offence!

Certification of the accounts effectively closes the period and provides a certificate of the expenditure and sometimes income relating to it. In some cases it is to be provided by the managing agent in others by an accountant.

In the residential sector provision to allow for accounts without an accountant's certificate but in the correct form and within the time scale may apply currently when there are fewer than five dwellings. This exception may be varied by statutory instrument, but not the requirement to provide accounts in the statutory form.

In the commercial sector leases may provide that the certificate shall be final and binding. This may limit your ability to recover further monies for the period at a later date should some error be discovered.

12.7 What does 'save as to manifest error' mean?

Effectively this means that while the accounts would be final in the normal run of events. If there is an obvious mistake, which should immediately be apparent, then this can be corrected.

12.8 Rights to inspect documents

In the commercial sector this right will be covered by the lease or an application to the court.

In the residential sector it follows on from section 21 of the LTA 1985 as amended. After accounts have been produced section 22 applies. The CLRA 2002 is altering things but basically there is a right to inspect invoices and other papers and a duty to provide facilities to make copies. The old requirement was for six months after production of the accounts and the new one is for 12 months after the year-end or 6 months after production of the accounts whichever is the longer.

Facilities must be provided free of charge with copying available (at a reasonable fee). The cost of providing the facilities may be charged to the service charge.

A section 23 LTA 1985 request may be made to provide information held by a superior landlord and again this must be complied with. If you receive such a request from a head-lessee you will need to comply with it.

12.9 External audit of accounts

As the authors have attempted to demonstrate service charge accounting differs in many ways from company or personal accounting. For those of us who enjoy mathematics it can be an enjoyable part of our work and the more complicated the schedules the more mentally stimulating the effort of achieving the correct result.

Do not forget that this is a specialised area of accounting and just as we need to know all the rules so does any accountant certifying or auditing our work. To gain the maximum advantage from the audit process the auditor needs to be experienced in the field.

From a professional point of view one would not wish to impede an auditor from doing whatever work he or she considers necessary or to seek to limit the fee to below that which he or she needs to undertake the job properly. On the other hand it is not reasonable to be expected to spend hours explaining the appropriate law or re-correcting alterations which have been made incorrectly to your accounts without being able to charge for the time involved.

When considering residential service charges the requirement for these to be reasonable should always be borne in mind – this includes professional fees.

From the client's point of view and that of the lessees, their interests are also best served by an experienced accountant in the field as he or she is more likely to be able to offer useful advice and spot any irregularities if the worst has happened.

All that said, from a professional point of view it may do you no harm at all to invest the necessary time in helping local auditors to gain experience in this field and at the same time benefit from their expertise in other spheres.

13

Residential rent, administration and service charge demands

This is yet another area in which the rules affecting the residential sector are far more draconian than those applying in the commercial sector. From October 2007 it is a criminal offence not to comply with some of them. This chapter will cover:

- Landlord's name and address to be contained in demands for rent, etc.
- Notification of landlord's address for service of notices
- Prescribed form of rent demand notice
- Service charges – summary of rights and obligations to accompany demands
- Administration charges – summary of rights and obligations to accompany demands

13.1 Landlord's name and address to be contained in demands for rent, etc.

Under section 47 of the LTA 1987 any written demand for rent or service charge needs to contain the landlords name and address and if that is not in England and Wales then an address in England and Wales for service upon the landlord of notices (including notices of proceedings).

If this information is omitted any part of the demand which includes service charges will not be due until a notice is served. This produced some interesting litigation which tried to argue that no service charge would be due for periods where faulty demands had been served but this was resolved by a ruling that once a notice was served the back demands would become due.

13.2 Notification of landlord's address for service of notices

Under section 48 of the LTA 1987 the landlord is required to furnish the tenant with an address in England & Wales for service of notices (including notices of proceedings). Rent and service charges are to be treated as not due until such a notice is served.

13.3 Prescribed form of rent demand notice

Under section 166 of the CLRA 2002 a tenant of a long leasehold dwelling is not liable to make a payment of rent unless the landlord has served upon him a notice in the prescribed form.

This must be sent not less than 30 days and not more than 60 days from the due date to the dwelling or to such other address as the tenant has nominated in writing in England and Wales.

This brings about some interesting problems in that an address for example in Scotland is not good enough. No action for default or penalty can be imposed until the notice has run its course and none can be applied for any period prior to the notice running its course. These notices can be served at a date after the contractual one but the rent only becomes due on the date in the notice.

To an extent one can take a view on the need for these notices if the rent is always paid on time but one is necessary to charge interest (which cannot be backdated) or carry out any form of recovery.

The text is set out in SI 2004/3096, the *Landlord and Tenant (Notice of Rent) (England) Regulations* 2004.

13.4 Service charges – summary of rights and obligations to accompany demands

Under Section 153 of CLRA 2002 a new section 21B of the LTA 1985 is inserted requiring a statement of rights and obligations to accompany every service charge demand. This statement is prescribed in SI 2007/1257, the *Service Charges (Summary of Rights and Obligations, and Transitional Provision) (England) Regulations* 2007.

It is very important to note that a failure to comply with this section is a criminal offence under section 24 of that Act. Whether or not legislators realised this when they voted for it is another matter but this is what they achieved.

In addition tenants are not liable to pay until they do receive the summary in the correct form and provisions for recovery cannot be followed until it has been sent.

13.5 Administration charges – summary of rights and obligations to accompany demands

Many charges are now covered in particular for granting licenses and charging for reminders. Some of these are essential and it is only right that the costs are borne by the beneficiaries rather than the service charge as a whole but you do need to think about the reasonableness of charges before you make them. For some firms this may mean a revision up as well as down and an assessment of exactly what some tasks really do cost.

Under Schedule 11 of the CLRA 2002 the reasonableness of administration charges is addressed and under 4(2) a statement of rights and obligations to accompany every administration charge demand is imposed. This statement is prescribed in SI 2007/ 1258, the *Administration Charges (Summary of Rights and Obligations) (England) Regulations* 2007

Schedule 11 of the CLRA 2002 is intended to close the loophole by which excessive charges were rendered for matters of administration.

14

Dealing with and avoiding disputes

Whilst this chapter is divided between the commercial and residential sector, those practising in the commercial field may find some of the contents of the 'residential sector' helpful in its approach to solving problems and appreciating their causes. When the section was written it was not intended to be exclusively residential although much of its content is applicable to the rules governing the residential sector. The chapter discusses:

- The importance of records
- Disabilities
- Types of dispute
- What happens if the dispute can't be resolved by negotiation and information?
- Do the tenants have the right to withhold on-account payments?
- Withholding balancing charges due?
- The commercial sector

One of the main aims of management policy must be to avoid disputes occurring in the first place. When they do happen they are usually costly and at best this is restricted to the time spent dealing with them. It has been fashionable for some time to blame most problems on a lack of communication, but to be fair communications that are not understood (or highlight contentious matters without fully explaining them) can often be as likely to lead to disputes than no communication at all!

Not to say that providing information will not lead to a reduction in disputes, as if it is given promptly, in a form which can be clearly understood, a dispute based on misunderstanding can be avoided. The problem faced as managing agents is that tenants have varying ideas and expectations. In the residential sector the managing agent may have a far better idea of the priorities of resident lessees than of the non-residents – finding him or herself criticised by one group and praised by another. At the end of the day the managing agent must be seen by all sides to act fairly, diligently and competently if disputes are to be avoided

It is fairly inevitable that we will come across some tenants whose expectations are unrealistic or whose resources in terms of spare time are extensive and devoted to complaining about the most minor of matters. There is a temptation to ignore these people after attempting to meet their needs. While it may be necessary to put some limit on the time spent communicating with them this must be done in such a way as to ensure that any legitimate complaints are dealt with.

Within reason you might also consider the advantages of harnessing the underemployed resources of particular tenants to report problems and genuinely assist in the smooth management of a development.

14.1 The importance of records

Some of us are blessed with extremely good memories while others are not. It cannot be overemphasised that should there be any potential for a dispute written records should be kept. Perhaps the majority of disputes are caused by genuine misunderstanding and many people seem to remember what they wanted to hear rather than what was actually said. The ability to draw attention to copy correspondence will be invaluable should a dispute arise.

In the same vein the ability to refresh your own memory on a case, or effectively review it if it has been handled by others, may result in a better understanding of the other person's point of view and how they arrived at it. It may well be that this may lead to a reconsideration of the position and an amicable settlement.

It is possible particularly in residential developments for rumours which do not reflect the facts to be innocently spread. Here again written records can be used to confirm the reality of the situation.

14.2 Disabilities

It is very important to ensure that tenants with disabilities which may hinder communication are catered for. Deafness, sight problems and poor memory retention are not always obvious and many of the sufferers either do not admit to them or do not realise the extent of the problem. You should be aware of these potential problems and be proactive in providing solutions.

In this day and age a letter can be produced in large bold type with almost no extra effort.

14.3 Types of dispute

While the forms of dispute encountered may be various, they can be divided between those which involve our actions as managers or those of our clients, and those which occur between tenants. There is of course a third category involving third parties but we will not deal with them here.

Disputes between tenants

Disputes between tenants are not uncommon and the tenant can of course look to the managing agent as a first port of call. Increasingly leases are deemed defective if they do not provide for the landlord to enforce covenants (subject to a guarantee of his or her costs).

The managing agent's role in disputes may vary considerably depending upon exactly what is provided for within the leases. You will need to ensure that you are aware of their content and prepared to perform whatever role is appointed to you.

In these days where mediation is encouraged the range of dispute resolution is quite varied and will differ substantially from one development to another.

If you are entitled to your costs for resolving a dispute you should make it clear to the parties that this is the case and seek their confirmation that they will be paying your account. You may decide that some initial work will be covered within your general management fees (e.g. writing a letter or two or a brief discussion to clarify matters). It is probably wise to set out a protocol for dealing with these matters to ensure that there is a stage at which you will generally seek to recover costs.

It may be that tenants will be happy to continue a dispute if it is not costing them anything but consider it in a different light if they have to bear the costs of the argument. You will need to assess disputes on a case by case basis but are wise to be aware of the potential costs which can be expended dealing with them in terms of resources.

The ideal solution

While some disputes will unfortunately result in protracted proceedings many others may be settled fairly amicably by the good offices of the managing agent. Disputes in commercial property are usually undesirable and stressful but those in the residential sector between residents are generally much worse. This is because the parties cannot go home to escape the problem and relax as they would wish to. On the contrary the place where they should be able to relax becomes a place of stress. This often leads to a far greater determination and perhaps sometimes disproportionate obsession with a minor dispute. It also means that a major one can lead to ill health.

Over the years it has always been extremely rewarding to settle some of these disputes by discussing the matter with both parties involved. This solution will not always be possible but if you can, achieving it will generally be beneficial.

You should be careful not to appear to take sides particularly before you have discovered all the facts. While tenant A may well be contravening the lease by parking his or her commercial vehicle in the car park; tenant B, who complained, may be letting his or her children play football in the garden in clear breach of the lease. In fact they might both be doing various other things which annoy each other because they are breaking rules but haven't even raised the points. It is also probable that while the offenders realise that the other tenant objects they do not appreciate that they are in breach of their respective leases.

In cases like this a solution may be achieved by providing full details of lease covenants and regulations and insisting that they are complied with. On the other hand the suggestion that this is likely to happen might be equally effective!

Do not be surprised to discover that the complainant has not mentioned the problem to the culprit! On the other hand there may be a real fear of reprisal even if it is totally unjustified.

Be prepared to be firm but tactful and innovative.

Example

It is interesting that the majority of complaints about late night noise in some blocks of flats come from young working professionals kept awake by pensioners, suffering from hearing impairments and insomnia, watching the television in the early hours of the morning! They do not realise how loud it is and may well, despite their denials, regularly doze off. A set of comfortable earphones may keep everybody happy!

Disputes concerning the landlord or managing agent's actions

It is not at all uncommon for tenants to raise queries over the actions of the landlord or his or her managing agent. There are also varied reasons why this should happen. Firstly of course it may well be that something has not been done properly. In such a case a prompt apology and correction of the error together with an explanation of how it occurred will often be the end of the matter. It is important though that you should not admit to having done something in error when in fact you have not.

Disputes are also raised for the following reasons:

- inability to pay a bill;
- wish to delay payment of a bill;
- incorrect understanding of liability;
- incorrect understanding of a situation; and
- a wish to achieve an unrelated aim.

If disputes are to be settled it is essential that the cause is identified and any misunderstandings corrected.

It is not uncommon for a dispute over management to occur which results in non-payment of service charges. This can happen quite legitimately and those organising the tenants can be genuine in their aims. Once an amicable settlement is reached, which can often result in greater understanding on both sides, you may then be faced with a problem collecting charges from those tenants who regarded the dispute as a useful excuse to avoid payment.

146

Those who led the dispute are often surprised to discover that their recommendation to pay in order to move forward with the services which they agreed to and want has been ignored by this faction and as a result works are delayed.

14.4 What happens if the dispute cannot be resolved by negotiation and information?

Here again the residential and commercial sectors present different options.

In the residential sector we can refer disputes to the Leasehold Valuation Tribunal. This is supposed to be quicker and cheaper than a referral to court. The Leasehold Valuation Tribunal is dealt with in chapter 24. If things work well it does provide access to a decision on a disputed matter and It is open to a landlord to apply to the tribunal for a declaration that major expenditure would be reasonable before he or she incurs it.

If there is plenty of time and disagreement between parties over the way forward then you should consider an application to the Leasehold Valuation Tribunal. You do not have to brief a lawyer to conduct a case and can appear yourself. The RICS practice statement *Surveyors Acting as Expert Witnesses* will apply as will the forthcoming practice statement on surveyors acting as advocates. In both cases you should read the practice statements before you start as they lay down rules of conduct which must be adhered to.

On the other hand you will probably find yourself having to prepare trial bundles and comply with directions. The rules are not as strict as those for the courts which can be of assistance but may also be frustrating. If the dispute is complicated you will need to provide explanations and may need to draw the tribunal's attention to relevant case or statute law.

No system can be perfect but a great deal of preparation time can be wasted in a system where preliminary hearings are rare and heads of claim are not always struck out by the tribunal until the hearing date.

If you are comfortable attending tribunals, giving evidence and acting as an advocate, as well as being willing to deal with the paperwork involved, the Leasehold Valuation Tribunal may be very useful to you in resolving disputes before they escalate.

You can still issue proceedings for non-payment of residential service charges in the County Court and provided that there is no valid dispute it is probably sensible to do so. If however a defence is lodged the court will refer service charge disputes back to the Leasehold Valuation Tribunal. Only when the Leasehold Valuation Tribunal has determined the matter, or the tenant has admitted it, will it return to the court. There are severe limitations on recovery of costs from either party at a Leasehold Valuation Tribunal although costs may be charged to the service charge account if permitted under the lease terms – the tribunal may make an order limiting or preventing this.

Once a case has commenced it must be pursued, compromised or dropped. You will need to consider the possible consequences of a defended action before commencing it. The costs of a defended action may outweigh any benefit derived. You should consider the benefit of delaying action until arrears are above a certain level.

In the commercial sector leases may provide for alternative dispute resolution or reference to arbitrators or experts. It is important that you fully understand the provisions and the mechanism for following them. In some cases time may be of the essence and care should be taken to ensure that you comply with what is required.

If you arrive at a situation whereby you need to go to court you should ensure that you have a sound case or one which requires some form of order to clarify matters. Legal action can be extremely costly.

In all cases you should attempt to crystallise and minimise the areas of dispute. A great deal of court time can be wasted arguing relatively unimportant points.

14.5 Do the tenants have the right to withhold on-account payments?

The terms of most leases will contract the tenants to pay the service charges but this will not extend to charges which are clearly unreasonable. Here again the two sectors diverge. In practice the residential law prevents forfeiture for disputed service charges until a Leasehold Valuation Tribunal has determined that they are reasonable. Service charges must be reasonable and if they are not they are not recoverable. In addition any charge for non payment of an unreasonable demand will not be recoverable.

The situation is slightly different in the commercial sector as, unless the lease makes specific provision, there is no implied obligation that estimates should be reasonable – although a tenant may not be liable to pay a proportion of the on-account charges relating to items which are not recoverable under the lease.

Where a tenant does withhold payment and the service charge is reserved as rent there may be a clear risk of forfeiture for non-payment if the court determines that the demand was not improper. In practice however it is unusual for a landlord to seek to forfeit a lease where a genuine service charge dispute exists. In any event, if it is determined that the service charge is properly due, the tenant will usually have a period within which to pay the disputed amount and thus obtain relief.

Clearly in either case if the leases do not provide for the collection of on-account payments then they cannot be enforced. There is provision in the residential field to apply to a Leasehold Valuation Tribunal for a lease variation to allow for on-account charges but generally this would require the support of a substantial majority of the tenants before it could even be considered. This is different to the commercial sector where the terms of the lease are paramount and a tenant is under no obligation to make on-account service charge payments unless the lease makes specific provision.

As a general rule for both residential and commercial properties, the provision of services is not conditional on the payment of the service charge. Even if a tenant is in arrears the landlord will not be absolved from responsibility to provide services – although if a tenant wilfully withholds payment creating a situation whereby the landlord is unable to perform its covenants, the position will be different.

14.6 Withholding balancing charges due?

Balancing charges will not generally become due until the accounting requirements set out within the lease have been complied with. Those dealing with the commercial sector will be able to look to the leases for the requirements and while it must be seen to be desirable to get the accounts completed as soon as possible statute does little to intervene beyond the *Limitation Acts* (although the Code of Practice for *Service Charges in Commercial Property* now does).

The residential manager on the other hand has several time constraints and legislation which often overrides the lease provisions.

Unless a warning notice has been given expenditure cannot be recovered more than 18 months after it was incurred. This in itself may create an interesting argument in determining exactly when the expenditure was incurred. If service charges were demanded in advance then it will have been necessary to exhaust the on-account payment before such expenditure is incurred. This may well be towards the end of a service charge year rather than at the beginning. In addition as long as reserves are correctly used to fund expenditure it may not be necessary to recover that expenditure by a further demand. A future increased demand for additional reserves would merely reflect the current need to top-up the reserve fund.

If you are in a situation where charges are made in arrears clearly this constraint has more significance and unless you can get the charge out promptly it may be prudent to issue a warning notice.

As discussed there are clear statutory requirements for residential service charge accounting and unless these have been complied with it will either not be possible to enforce any demand for balancing charges or be highly unlikely that a Leasehold Valuation Tribunal will uphold them.

In all cases you will only be able to recover those costs allowed for within the leases or by statute. If you attempt to recover further sums for whatever reason you will run the risk of incurring the tenant's legal costs should you pursue the matter.

There are cases where agreements between lessees and tenants have led to sums being recovered which are not strictly due under the leases. If you are a party to such an agreement you should ensure that consent to it in writing is obtained from all concerned or that your clients are made aware of the situation and possible consequences. Generally these situations come about as a result of tenant demand and willingness to pay but run into trouble when someone changes their mind or takes an assignment. Lessee-owned management companies are often keen to set their own rules but you should consider the implications of not warning them of any possible future consequences.

14.7 The commercial sector

Unless the lease provides for any disputes to be referred either to an arbitrator or an expert the tenant of commercial premises is required to have recourse to the courts to determine disputes. Obviously this can be a lengthy and expensive process and often the cost of pursuing a claim can far outweigh the actual amounts in dispute.

The *Civil Procedure Rules* (Woolfe Reforms) which came into effect in April 1999 have had a major impact on the way in which civil litigation is conducted in the courts in England and Wales and encourage pre-litigation negotiation and settlement.

The new RICS Code of Practice for *Service Charge in Commercial Leases* also encourages people to resolve their disputes without the intervention of the courts; providing access to alternative dispute resolution (ADR) for parties involved in disputes about service charge matters.

The attitude adopted by the courts is that litigation should be seen as a last resort and from April 2006, the courts take into account whether the parties have given proper consideration to the use of ADR, a party failing to give proper consideration to the use of ADR can be penalised in costs even if it wins at trial.

Through the Code RICS has established a trained panel of service charge experts to provide impartial and expert determination of disputes. The benefits of expert determination are that the dispute is resolved relatively quickly, is informal and private, and the decision is made by a neutral expert who knows the subject matter intimately.

15

Interest on service charge accounts

15.1 The residential sector

This is covered by section 42 of the LTA 1987 which sets out the manner in which service charges must be held in trust. The CLRA 2002 sets out to create a further requirement to operate separate bank accounts for each property or schedule within a property however at the time of writing that requirement had not come into force. Exactly what happens remains to be seen not least as the cost implications may be substantial in some cases.

15.2 The commercial sector

It has become a growing trend over recent years for tenants to request advance service charge payments to be held in separate interest bearing accounts with interest earned credited to the benefit of the tenants.

Leases will often enable the landlord to recover the cost of borrowing to fund major non-cyclical expenditure, which would fall as a cost to the service charge. Many tenants believe that the payment of on-account service charges results in a positive net cash flow for landlords and it would not therefore be unreasonable to expect interest earned to be credited to the service charge account.

Positive or negative cash flow will be dependent upon the timing of proposed expenditure. Above average monthly expenditure, incurred in respect of such items as energy or Christmas decorations and promotions during winter months may be balanced out by the cost of maintenance and repair orks carried out at other times of the year when more clement weather would be a factor in the timing of such works. However, significant non-cyclical expenditure may be incurred which could result in a positive or negative net cash flow dependant upon the timing of the expenditure in relation to the service charge period.

The crediting of interest to the service charge account is a vexed issue principally because, in the majority of commercial leases, the service charge is reserved as rent. In essence, the income is the landlord's to do with as he or she will. However the landlord is still required to perform obligations under the terms of the lease to provide the services, and to account to tenants for any balancing charges due or owed in respect of actual expenditure incurred at the end of the service charge period.

Where a managing agent is employed for the management of a centre, and separate client bank accounts are maintained in order to comply with RICS client accounting rules, it may be relatively easy for the advance service charges to be separately identified.

However, in the absence of any contrary wording in the lease, the existence of a separate client account cannot be considered, per se, as obliging the landlord to credit interest earned to the benefit of the occupiers.

Notwithstanding the RICS accounting rules that govern how managing agents are to account for client income; the landlord is often under no contractual obligation to retain advance service charge payments in a separate bank account. Many landlords will manage their own property portfolios directly, or through a management company, in which case the RICS accounting rules will not apply. Accordingly, the landlord may not be able to readily separate advance service charge payments from other income receipts.

In such circumstances, while the landlord might in theory benefit from a positive cash flow, he or she also bears the risk of funding any shortfall as a result of a theoretical negative cash flow.

In practice however the interest that might accrue to a service charge account is often out-weighed by the cost of bank charges for administering separate accounts.

However, where there is a contractual obligation on the part of the landlord to hold advance service charge payments in a separate interest bearing account, the lease provisions creating this obligation will need to be carefully considered and will require precise drafting. If the tenants are to receive the benefit of interest earned as a result of positive cash flow in equity, they should also bear the cost of funding any negative cash flow.

Interest charged to and received from tenants for late payment of service charges should also be credited to the service charge account. However, the costs incurred in respect of matters between the owner and individual occupiers are not usually regarded as costs which should be included in the service charge account (e.g. enforcement of covenants for collection of rent, which would include advance service charge payments). Such costs may not always be wholly recoverable and therefore should the service charge account also bear the costs of pursuing recovery of late payment by tenants? This is potentially inconsistent with established good practice.

The contribution to the service charge account in respect of void units will also create problems. The landlord is likely to be required to fund the contribution in respect of void units where previously these would have been treated as a deduction against total net income.

There are further issues with regard to the treatment of VAT and tax that create complications (i.e. should the account be net or gross of VAT and who pays the tax on interest earned, and at what rate?) HM Revenue and Customs is likely to regard on-account payments received as direct landlord income and will therefore deal with the VAT and tax accordingly.

Finally, management fees may also come under pressure to increase, as the landlord or managing agent will want to recover the additional administrative costs of operating separate bank accounts.

It is the authors opinion that the issue of interest on service charge accounts is similar in many ways to that of sinking funds – while laudable in theory, the associated tax and administrative problems and costs may, in practice outweigh the benefits.

However the RICS Code of Practice for *Service Charges in Commercial Property* recommends as best practice that the service charge should be cash neutral to the owners income stream. It therefore supports the crediting of interest earned on service charge accounts to the service charge and that modern leases should also enable owners to recover the cost of borrowing to fund major non-cyclical expenditure as a cost to the service charge.

Notwithstanding the precise terms of the occupational leases, to ensure transparency it is good practice that owners should clearly state their policy with regard to the crediting of interest to the service charge when communicating with tenants through budget and actual expenditure reports.

16

Replacement funds and depreciation charges

16.1 The residential sector

The residential sector is governed by a raft of legislation to ensure that contributions are reasonable and justified. In effect this means that while the reserve fund approach as defined below can and if possible should be used, the methods set out in the commercial sector are not generally applicable to the residential sector. Section 42 of the LTA 1987 sets out the final ownership of the fund. If there is no provision for a reserve fund within the leases consideration should be given to making an application to the Leasehold Valuation Tribunal to have one set up. You should remember that the tribunal can be asked to determine the reasonableness of costs including contributions to reserves.

Reserve funds

The RICS *Service Charge Residential Management Code* defines a reserve fund as:

> '... a pool of money created to build up sums which can be used to pay for large items of infrequent expenditure (such as the replacement of a lift or the recovering of a roof) and for major items which arise regularly (such as redecoration). A reserve fund also helps to spread costs between successive Leaseholders/Tenants and can, if the lease/ tenancy agreement allow, be used to fund the cost of routine services, avoiding the need to borrow money.'

If the reserve fund is not adequately funded you should always consider transferring any year-end surpluses to it. A landlord is only entitled to apply monies to a reserve fund which are fair and reasonable. This may mean that commercial property is treated in a very different way to residential, not least because of the term of the leases involved and the ultimate beneficiary of the fund. The terms of the lease setting up the reserve fund will have to be adhered to, in so far as they do not conflict with statute. If the lease sets out conditions for assessing or certifying the fund they must be followed.

In *St Mary's Mansions Ltd v Limegate Investments Co. Ltd* the reserve fund was certified by an accountant and the landlord then attempted to transfer the year-end surplus in addition to the certified requirement to the reserve fund. The court held that:

> A landlord is only entitled to apply monies to a reserve fund which are fair and reasonable and in respect of specifically identified expenditure for which the reserve fund was created rather than other, unidentified, future expenses. A landlord cannot arbitrarily transfer a surplus in the on-account service charge payments made by tenants to a reserve fund.

Section 18 of the LTA 1985 defines service charges as:

> '... an amount payable by a tenant of a dwelling as part of or in addition to the rent –

(a) which is payable directly or indirectly for services, repairs, maintenance *improvements (CLRA 2002)* or insurance or the landlords cost of management and

(b) the whole or part of which varies or may vary according to the relevant costs. The relevant costs are the costs or estimated costs incurred **or to be incurred** by or on behalf of the landlord or a superior landlord in connection with the matters for which the service charge is payable.'

Section 42 of the LTA 1987 places a statutory requirement for the investment of monies received as trust funds. The CLRA 2002 (section 156) includes a new section 42A of the LTA 1987 which provides that service charge contributions (including sinking fund contributions) in respect of residential dwellings are to be held in trust in a designated account with a relevant institution. At the time of writing the old section 42 still applied as there has been a delay in enacting section 42A.

From the above it can be seen that reserve funds and sinking funds in the residential sector are generally descriptions widely used for the same purpose. This is not the case in the commercial sector.

16.2 The commercial sector

The service charge provisions of many commercial leases will often provide for the expenses and outgoings incurred by the landlord to include a sum or sums of money by way of 'provision' for anticipated future expenditure, such amount to be determined by the landlord in his or her reasonable discretion.

Some leases are more specific in providing that the service charge may include making such provision for a reserve fund for anticipated expenditure in respect of the future provision of the services specified in the lease, or for the establishment of a sinking fund for the replacement of certain plant and equipment.

Sinking funds and reserve funds (which for ease of reference we shall refer to collectively as replacement funds) and depreciation charges are often confused with one another.

Basic principles

A tenant will only be liable to contribute towards a replacement fund or to pay a depreciation charge so far as the lease provides.

Landlords of multi-let commercial buildings will often find themselves providing a multiplicity of services to tenants. These will include, amongst other things the maintenance, repair and renewal of plant and equipment for the provision of a lift service, heating, air-conditioning etc. and the repair and maintenance of the fabric (e.g. roofs, walls, foundations, etc.).

Therefore, during the life cycle of a building, the landlord may be required to replace large items of equipment or fabric, the cost of which might be recoverable from the tenant through the service charge. These large replacements of equipment or fabric do not occur very frequently, but when they do can involve disproportionately high expenditure compared with the year-on-year running costs for a building.

The basic purpose of a 'reserve fund' or 'sinking fund' is to provide for maintenance and repair work on the common parts of leased property which are likely to result in substantial one-off payments.

The landlord has the advantage of having funds on which to draw to pay for such work. The advantage to the tenant is that they are not required to meet their proportion of the costs of the work in one lump sum in any one year in which substantial work is carried out.

Instead, the tenants' contributions to the sinking or reserve fund effectively spread the costs over a period.

The terms 'sinking fund' and 'reserve fund' are often used interchangeably, however, they are not quite synonymous and there is an important distinction between them.

Sinking funds

A sinking fund is a replacement fund by which the landlord aims to build up a fund to pay for repair and replacement of major items of fabric, plant and equipment. The fund would usually be accumulated over the anticipated life of the item and may often therefore include costs that might be expended beyond the term of the occupation leases.

Lift and heating plant might reasonably have a life expectancy of anything from 20–25 years, but it is not unusual for this to be extended dependant upon the quality of the original installation and a comprehensive and pro-active maintenance regime.

Given that modern leases are granted for an average of 10–15 years, a modern building might see leases renewed a number of times before the need for major expenditure has occurred. In the case of shorter leases or where leases are not renewed, expenditure might be incurred many years after the contractual expiry date.

In such circumstances the tenants in occupation of the building at the time the major expenditure was incurred, would bear the cost. However, this is viewed by many to be unfair or iniquitous if a tenant that enjoyed the benefit of the services for 20–25 years vacated just prior to the need for replacement, thereby avoiding any liability for the replacement of the item, while a tenant who took a new lease much later in the life-cycle of the building might be liable for a substantial cost.

Reserve funds

A reserve fund is intended to equalise expenditure in respect of regularly recurring items so as to avoid fluctuations in the amount of service charge payable each year, for example, internal or external redecorations, which might be carried out, say, every five years.

The important distinction between sinking funds and reserve funds arises from the implication that tenants are usually only liable for actual expenditure incurred during the term of the lease. Therefore, while a sinking fund might be intended for large replacement items which might occur after the expiry date of the lease, a reserve fund, intended to even out the tenant's service charge liability from year-to-year, should only include costs of works or services that are anticipated during the term of the lease.

However, most leases do not provide clarity to clearly distinguish between sinking funds and reserve funds and in the absence of any wording in the lease, it has hitherto been assumed that there is unlikely to be any implied obligation on behalf of the landlord to repay any unexpended balance of any reserve fund held by the landlord upon expiry of the lease.

A very recent Court of Appeal decision has provided some much needed clarity in this area.

In the case of *Brown's Operating Systems v Southwark Roman Catholic Diocesan Corporation* [2007] it was held that in the absence of a clear provision that sums collected from tenants for future expenditure are to belong to the landlord, or must be held in a separate reserve fund, a tenant was entitled to any unexpended monies held at the end of the lease.

The decision in this case also reinforced the definition and interpretation of a reserve fund in that the court considered that the contributions were only intended to cover expenditure reasonably required **during the lease** and did not create a fund designed to cover the obligations which the landlord would have to meet at some future time, possibly after the expiry of the current lease.

It is therefore important that the lease should be specific as to whether the parties intend for a sinking fund or a reserve fund (or both) to be created.

Depreciation

A depreciation charge (often incorrectly referred to as a depreciation 'fund') is in effect, the reverse of a replacement fund.

Fixed assets have a finite useful economic life (i.e. the period over which its owner can derive economic benefit from its use).

Depreciation is the measure of the wearing out, consumption or other reduction in life of the asset. A depreciation provision in the service charge clause of a lease will enable the landlord to include an amount to reflect this 'cost' of the annual depreciation of the plant and equipment.

The monies received by way of depreciation have been held to belong to the landlord absolutely (*Secretary of State for the Environment v Possfund (North West) Ltd* [1997]). However, when plant and equipment reaches the end of its economic life, and needs to be replaced, it would be for the landlord to fund the replacement costs entirely from its own resources. Upon replacement of the equipment, the landlord would continue to charge tenants the depreciation of the new plant, and the cycle would continue.

Ownership of the funds

Unlike residential property, there is no legislation governing funds which arise under commercial leases. In commercial leases the question of 'ownership' of the fund will depend on the terms of the lease.

The service charge is frequently reserved as additional rent and the sinking or reserve fund contributions have generally been considered to belong to the landlord – although dependant upon the specific circumstances and the wording of the lease, they might be treated as if they form part of an implied or constructed trust.

A trust is formed where there is a separation in beneficial ownership from legal ownership.

Where a replacement fund is held in trust this provides protection to the funds in the event of a liquidation of the landlord, and also ensures that the funds are treated, for tax purposes, as a trust, which can be more beneficial than if the fund belongs wholly to the landlord.

If a lease does not specify the basis on which the fund is to be held, the 'ownership' of the fund will be determined as a question of fact. Where a lease makes no provision that sums collected from tenants are to belong to the landlord, or must be held in a separate reserve fund, the tenant is entitled to any unexpended monies held at the end of the lease.

Advantages of replacement funds

The basic purpose of a 'reserve fund' or ' sinking fund' is to provide for maintenance and repair work on the common parts of leased property which are likely to result in substantial one-off payments such as the replacement of major items of fabric, plant and equipment (a sinking fund) or more frequent cyclical repair and redecorations (a reserve fund).

These large replacements of equipment or fabric do not occur very frequently, but when they do can involve disproportionately high expenditure compared with the year on year running costs for a building.

The landlord has the advantage of having funds on which to draw to pay for such work. The advantage to the tenant is that they are not required to meet their proportion of the costs of the work in one lump sum in any one year in which substantial work is carried out.

Instead, the tenants' contributions to the sinking or reserve fund effectively spread the costs over a period.

While benefiting tenant cash flow, the replacement fund also provides the landlord with the financial resource to fund work without the need to borrow money, which in itself may not be recoverable from tenants as part of the service charge.

In principle therefore, sinking funds or reserve funds appear to be a good idea in theory. However, the disadvantages, particularly from the tenants' perspective, and the onerous tax and administrative burdens associated with them will often outweigh any benefit.

Disadvantages of replacement funds

Many tenants are, perhaps understandably, wary of replacement funds.

Tenants may not see the benefit of their contributions into a replacement fund if they assign the lease or vacate the premises before the need for major expenditure occurs.

Where the replacement fund is not held formally in trust, a tenant risks becoming an unsecured creditor if the landlord becomes insolvent.

Where a lease is granted, for example in excess of 25 years, and it can reasonably be anticipated that the replacement or other work for which the fund is intended is likely to be required during the term, the principle of the sinking fund works well.

However, difficulties can arise when shorter-term leases are granted. A tenant taking a five-year lease might reasonably object to contributing to expenditure which may not be necessary for many years following the expiration of the lease. Similarly, a tenant taking a short lease in an older building, might object to making contributions towards the replacement of equipment when they have only received benefit for a relatively short while.

Replacement funds also give rise to significant tax and administrative problems. As the service charge is reserved as rent, the payments made by tenants will be taxable in the landlord's hands in the same way as the principle rent, as will any interest earned on accumulated funds.

But holding the money in a trust account does not completely remove the problems. HM Revenue and Customs have taken the view that the payments made by tenants into a trust fund, if properly constituted, are capital in nature. In these circumstances the payment by the tenant would also be treated as capital and the tenant would be unable therefore to claim a tax deduction in its own Schedule A contribution. This would increase the tenant's tax burden and in some situations may outweigh the benefit and protection afforded by holding funds in trust.

There are also further issues concerning capital allowances, and who can legitimately claim them, when the funds are held in a capital trust. However, as these involve complex tax calculations it is not intended to go into further detail here and advice should always be sought from a competent tax specialist.

Overcoming the problems

Many tenant concerns with regard to sinking and reserve funds can be overcome by ensuring that the lease stipulates:

- that any monies are to be held in a formally constituted trust account on behalf of the landlord and the tenants of the building from time-to-time;
- the purpose of the fund (i.e. for the replacement of the lift, heating plant, external redecoration, roof replacement etc.) In such circumstances the lease should be specific although there is no reason why a lease cannot provide an exhaustive list of items;
- that the landlord must act reasonably in estimating the amount of the contributions due and ideally should set out the basis of calculating the charge;
- by differentiating clearly between 'a reserve fund' and 'a sinking fund' in that the reserve fund is intended for items of expenditure that are anticipated will be carried out during the term of the lease, and the sinking funds for major items of plant and equipment and fabric; and
- that in the case of reserve funds, the tenant is to be reimbursed any excess monies collected and that remain unspent at the expiration of the lease.

Accounting for sinking and reserve funds

Where sinking funds and reserve funds are operated, budget reports issued to tenants should incorporate a clear statement on the amount included in the service charge, the purpose for the funds creation, whether the fund is held in trust and how interest earned on the account is treated.

Very often interest earned on a sinking fund is credited on a landlord basis to the service charge account. However, this is often treated somewhat suspiciously as it can be seen as a device to reduce the annual service charge bill. The interest should be accrued into the sinking fund account and therefore used to reduce the annual contributions required from tenants.

Calculation of the sinking and reserve fund contributions

It is generally held that such funds should be assessed annually by an independent professional surveyor or engineer, and by reference to the estimated life of plant or buildings and their likely eventual replacement cost.

In practice, however, it would be reasonable for the replacement cost to be assessed, say, every three years to avoid incurring additional and unnecessary fees.

The fund should be separately identified and run with buildings. In the event the landlord disposes of its interest in the property the fund should be either transferred to the purchaser or returned to the tenants.

Dependent always upon the precise wording of the lease, a landlord is generally only entitled to apply monies to a fund which are fair and reasonable and in respect of specifically identified expenditure for which the fund was created or intended, rather than other unidentified future expenses. A landlord cannot arbitrarily transfer a surplus in the on-account service charge payments made by tenants to a reserve or sinking fund.

Furthermore, when establishing a reserve or sinking fund, the landlord should only seek to build up a fund sufficient to meet the reasonably anticipated costs of future major repairs or replacements for which the fund is intended. Collection of excess monies, whether intentional or not, should be avoided.

The replacement fund should be capable of annual audit and certification.

Advantages of depreciation charges for commercial property

It is the authors' view that a depreciation charge has distinct advantages over a replacement fund. They are simpler to administer, and have neither the trust fund implications nor tax complications associated with replacement funds. They do, however, provide increased flexibility in respect of the length of leases granted, while ensuring that the landlord is not left with significant shortfalls when faced with major replacement works.

Because the contributions reflect an actual cost to the landlord, tenants who occupy buildings throughout the lifecycle of major plant would, in effect, pay for its ultimate replacement. Technically this places tenants in no worse a financial position than had they been liable for the total cost of replacement at the appropriate time or if contributions had been paid into a sinking fund.

The contributions belong to the landlord absolutely while there are no trust implications.

Because the depreciation charge reflects an actual cost, assessed annually, to the landlord, they can be used for both short- and long-term leases. The tenant who takes a short lease and vacates prior to the point at which at which major plant items require replacement, and a tenant who takes a lease later in the life cycle of the building would similarly contribute towards the ultimate replacement cost in proportion to their period of occupation, but would not be liable for the entire cost purely as a result of bad timing.

Because the depreciation charge belongs to the landlord absolutely, and the landlord is liable for the cost of replacing the equipment, the landlord would have a vested interest in extending the life of the plant and equipment. The landlord would wish to ensure that the building is maintained to a good standard to maximise its life, which would avoid the spurious replacements of plant and equipment, particularly near the end of relatively long-term leases.

17

Insurance

Insurance is a field in which there is now considerable statutory intervention and for once it is not limited to the residential sector although it almost goes without saying that there is a long set of additional rules governing residential work. This chapter discusses:

- FSA
- Lessee right to various documentation
- Right for tenant to notify insurers
- Leasehold Valuation Tribunal
- Commission and discounts
- What needs to be included
- The sum insured
- Pitfalls to avoid
- Rebuilding cost valuations

17.1 FSA

Recent developments have resulted from the implementation of an EU directive and most areas of insurance are now regulated by the Financial Services Authority (FSA). Unfortunately as the FSA does not generally deal with management of property it appears to have generated its regulations based on what it was used to dealing with and in some cases they may appear to chartered surveyors totally inappropriate.

Designated professional body

Having realised the burden FSA regulation would be placing on its members, RICS has now become a designated professional body (DPB) enabling it to regulate members in this field on behalf of the FSA. Members wishing to practice in this area who are not regulated by the FSA must apply for regulation by RICS.

It is very important to note that if you are carrying on almost any type of work involving selling or administering insurance, for clients, by way of business, then you must be regulated. This includes filling in claim forms and proposal forms or advising on insurance matters. It also includes referring business to brokers.

In practice if you wish to do any more than collect a premium arranged by your client's broker you will need to consider whether or not you need to be regulated. In the FSA documentation it even suggests that if you used a power of attorney for a client to execute insurance business you would require regulation!

On reflection this probably stems from the practice of stock brokers using these instruments on a more regular basis, but it illustrates the extent to which the FSA regulates.

It is hoped that RICS regulation will enable most firms to continue to work in this field to the benefit of all concerned. There had been a real problem for smaller agents who simply could not afford to comply with the FSA regulations. In the past they had administered claims and kept themselves aware of developments.

It is very difficult to see how allowing a third party to take all insurance responsibility could be in the best interests of landlords or tenants. This is particularly relevant when ensuring that claims are dealt with and repairs executed in the most appropriate manner.

17.2 Lessee's right to various documentation

Section 30 of the LTA 1985 implements the schedule to the Act 'Rights of Tenants with Respect to Insurance'.

Where a tenant is responsible for paying directly or indirectly for insurance he or she may require the landlord to provide a written summary of the insurance.

168

This may be handled on the tenants' behalf by the secretary of a recognised residents association, using the following process:

- the notice may be served upon an agent or person receiving the rent on behalf of the landlord who must pass it to the landlord;
- the landlord must comply within one month; and
- the summary must include:

    - the insured amount (this must include the whole building and if specified separately in the policy that for any flat to which the request refers);

    - the name of the insurer; and

    - the risks insured.

Alternatively the landlord may supply copies of any relevant policies.

If other buildings are covered within a policy they need not be included in the summary provided the above information is included.

Stage 2: further rights

Following receipt of the summary there is a further right within six months for the tenant to serve a written notice requiring facilities to inspect and take copies of:

- any relevant policy; or
- any accounts, receipts or other documents which provide evidence of any premiums due under any such policy in respect of the period of insurance which is current when the request is made and the period of insurance immediately preceding that period.

This should provide an extremely powerful incentive to ensure that demands reflect the actual premium paid and that if commissions are taken that they are reasonable. It is surprising that it is not used far more by lessee's representatives.

Given that the power deals with flats and the building which they are in, it enables lessees to confirm exactly how premiums are being split.

Superior landlords

Requests for summaries must be passed on by intermediate landlords and the summaries forwarded to the tenants when received.

If a request to inspect is then received then the immediate landlord must supply the superior landlords name and address to the tenant who may then serve the notice direct.

Failure to comply with any of the above is a criminal offence.

Right for tenant to notify insurers and limits to notification periods in policies

The tenant also has rights under section 30 of the LTA 1985 to inform the insurer direct of any potential claim in situations where there is a time limit for giving notice and the Act may have an effect on that time limit.

It would appear that the Act effectively extends any notification period to a minimum of six months where the tenant serves the appropriate notice on the insurer.

Right to challenge nominated insurers

The schedule of section 30 also confers rights to challenge nominated insurers at Leasehold Valuation Tribunals.

Insurance of leasehold houses

Section 164 of the CLRA 2002 has given lessees of dwelling houses as opposed to flats the right to serve notice that they will be using an alternate insurer.

If you wish to exercise this right or it is exercised it is necessary to comply with the terms of the Act.

Generally this is not a service charge matter but you may be involved in this field if you are administering a rent charge on a private estate or collect insurance from leasehold houses for any other reason. You may for example have a few houses tacked onto a flat development.

17.3 Leasehold Valuation Tribunals

Lessees have rights to challenge nominated insurers and insurance matters at a Leasehold Valuation Tribunal.

This should not be seen as an unfettered right to ensure that the insurance is the cheapest available but a right to ensure that the landlord has acted reasonably. The two are certainly not the same thing.

There is a tendency for insurance companies to cherry pick the market at present and offer cheap insurance to individuals often based on the fact that they have had no claims over the last few years and represent a low risk. This type of insurance rarely reflects the requirements of a policy for a block of flats yet the average lessee, who will probably not understand the situation fully, may well feel that he or she is being over charged.

Unfortunately this may result in an application to the Leasehold Valuation Tribunal by the lessee which may be time consuming and wasteful in terms of resources. It may well be necessary to let the procedure run its course and determine the matter even if your actions have been totally reasonable. This will certainly be more desirable than ending up with a sub-standard insurance.

It is worth considering the fact that if you compromise and allow a sub-standard situation then other lessees may seek to take action against you if a claim is not paid in full or at all. This would be far more difficult if your decision resulted from a Leasehold Valuation Tribunal determination.

The Leasehold Valuation Tribunal is set up not only to resolve disputes but to give decisions upon what actions may be deemed to be reasonable. If there is any significant doubt you may make an application to confirm that your proposed actions will be deemed reasonable.

To an extent there is a problem with the Leasehold Valuation Tribunal system in that its decisions have no precedence (cannot be taken to set the rules for future decisions). That being said previous decisions are quoted in cases and clearly have some weight. The tribunal will seek to reach a fair result and the facts in each case will affect the decision.

It has been decided in the past that the general commercial rates of major insurers were not deemed by the Leasehold Valuation Tribunal making the decision unreasonable even though they were above what the lessees could achieve elsewhere.

In another case a developer had obtained insurance for an estate and marketed the flats concerned indicating the rates applicable at the time in his estimate of the service charge. A lessee-owned management company was set up to run the estate with the nomination for insurance resting with the freeholders. The freehold was sold in several different parts covering individual blocks. One of the purchasers sought to nominate an insurer whose premium was in excess of double that charged by the original insurer who was willing to continue at the existing rates. The Leasehold Valuation Tribunal ruled that the landlord could continue to insure but that the recoverable premium could not exceed that which was available from the original broker or any other broker nominated by the lessee management company.

On receiving this ruling the new freeholders insurer then reduced its premium to that offered by the original insurers which to be fair was a highly competitive one. You should not expect to guarantee such a result in all cases and the circumstances were ones where a change which would enhance the freeholder's commission income was at stake. It does however call into question how a major insurance company was able to reduce its premium by such a large sum.

In general it is not unreasonable for a landlord to seek to insure through one major source not least to streamline administration and claims handling. There are often clear benefits to all concerned especially if the service offered is a better one. Generally the Leasehold Valuation Tribunal will only intervene if the costs involved become unreasonable and the individual tribunals will decide that for themselves.

Appeal from a Leasehold Valuation Tribunal

The appeal from the Leasehold Valuation Tribunal is to the Lands Tribunal.

17.4 Commission and discounts

Commissions and discounts should be declared to clients and tenants.

The original intention of insurance commission was to cover the costs involved in running an insurance business and to make a reasonable profit. For many years this system worked very well. It is quite clear that there are costs involved in collecting premiums, dealing with claims and otherwise administering insurance business.

Unfortunately as is so often the case the situation was exploited and it is somewhat ironic to note that the public sector in the shape of some local authorities was found to be taking a commission in one celebrated case of 70 per cent of the premium. Some large insurers argued that this merely reflected wholesale rates but in reality the situation could not be justified.

In many cases reasonable commissions are necessary to administer insurance and the alternative is to levy charges for administration if the leases permit.

You must take great care with the wording in leases as in some cases the landlord is only permitted to recover the **actual cost of the insurance incurred**. This means that the landlord may only be able to recover the premium net of any discounts or commissions, which cannot be added to the cost.

17.5 What needs to be included?

It is not the purpose of this book to advise how insurance work should be undertaken as this is a specialist regulated field. Without prejudice to the generality of the following you will need to deal with:

- **Employers liability insurance** – If anyone is directly employed by you or your client you must have an employer's liability policy in force.
- **Public liability insurance** – You will need sufficient public liability insurance on properties which you manage to cover claims in this field. As settlements increase and litigation and compensation increase the level of cover required will inevitably increase.

- **Buildings insurance** – This is of course self explanatory but do make sure that the policy covers those parts of the estate which are not part of individual demises, e.g. car park walls and lamp posts.
- **Contents insurance** – While you are probably not involved in insuring the contents of individual demises do not forget to insure contents of common parts, e.g. carpets, furniture and light fittings.

It may also be worth negotiating terms to insure carpets, etc. which belong to your clients in unrented property. While a tenant may be responsible for insuring items when he or she holds a lease these items may inadvertently become uninsured at a lease end or in a void period. This is not a service charge matter but worth considering.

- **Engineering insurance** – This is a specialist field and certain other activities which are not in fact insurance have become associated with it. These activities include lift inspections.

It is a statutory requirement to have lifts inspected at prescribed intervals. These inspections are carried out by a qualified person generally employed by an insurance company. There is a further statutory duty to act on the inspector's recommendations.

Historically the current situation has evolved because insurance companies carried out inspections in order to insure and maintain insurance on engineering plant. At one time there was a VAT advantage to having a policy which covered virtually nothing but carried out the statutory inspections as well. The VAT situation has changed but the connection with the insurance companies remains.

Unfortunately there can be some confusion where Lift Insurance is shown on a service charge yet the insurance element is negligible. In the same vein if you have a fully comprehensive lift contract you should confirm whether or not it is necessary to have full engineering insurance or whether the lift contract could be discounted as a result.

Engineering insurance is also available for other forms of plant and may be desirable.

- **Legal expenses cover** – Increasingly, cover for legal expenses is available and it is well worth considering this, but if you have it be careful to follow the policy conditions.

- **Employment insurance** – If you are employing staff the costs of adverse Employment Tribunal decisions may be significant. It is worth considering a policy to cover these but again be careful to follow the policy conditions to the letter.
- **Directors' insurance** – This is particularly relevant where a lessee management company runs a development. If you take out one of these policies, take care to ensure that the leases allow you to recover the costs as this is not always the case. Although these policies may cover defence costs they are unlikely to cover fines and will not prevent criminal convictions. As the emphasis of the law moves from the civil to the criminal director's liabilities have changed as indeed have those of a company secretary particularly in relation to health and safety matters.

17.6 The sum insured

There are at least three ways of expressing the buildings sum insured in a policy and it is important that you have some understanding of them as a misunderstanding could lead to a property either being under-insured or a significant excess premium being paid. Interestingly they all start from the same valuation.

You could insure for:

- a set sum and build into this an estimate for inflation during the period of insurance and subsequent reinstatement period;
- a fixed sum on an inflation guarded basis with a policy which will cover inflation linked to a specified index;
- a declared value at 'day one' which is uplifted by a percentage to cover the maximum liability which may occur under the policy, typically 150 per cent of the day one value. Please note however that the uplift may be less or more; or
- there are hybrids of the above and no doubt other methods available.

If you take on new management or swap insurers you need to ensure that the new insurance uses the right base figure correctly adjusted or you risk the possibility of an error occurring. In the past some large property companies were able to negotiate high percentage increases over the day-one value for very little extra premium. If this is 200 per cent and you use it as the basis for a basic inflation guarded policy the sum insured may be near to twice what it needs to be.

17.7 Pitfalls to avoid

These can be summarised as under- and over-insurance, and no insurance! The sections on engineering insurance and the sum insured illustrate how this can happen.

If an error has occurred do not automatically assume the worse before checking the situation. If for example a building had a poor claims history, it is possible that a minimum premium was placed on it. The sum insured might be double what it should have been but that may not be the case for the premium.

Look into the possibility of a policy to cover your errors and omissions. Always follow the policy conditions. When dealing with legal expenses cover and employment cover in particular you must follow the rules set down (in the latter advice will be given on notices, etc. which must be followed).

17.8 Rebuilding cost valuations

The Building Cost Information Service (BCIS) publishes a guide to house rebuilding costs and a guide to flat rebuilding costs as well as their more detailed elemental tables. Rebuilding cost valuations can be carried out by chartered surveyors using these. The guides contain a wealth of extremely useful information and elemental costs to cover different ages, types and regions.

A few hours spent studying the *House and Flat Guides* should enable a chartered surveyor to carry out the rebuilding cost valuations covered by these two volumes. They both contain relatively short but detailed guidance on the knowledge required which added to qualification requirements will equip you well for this task.

It is useful to note that the figures used by most loss adjusters to calculate claims and assess adequacy of insurance are derived from a simplified form of these tables. If you have a problem after the event a detailed calculation using the full BCIS tables may be of assistance.

18

Performance management contracts

These are generally relevant to the commercial sector although many of the principles are equally valid in the residential field. **Residential agents would need to consider section 20 LTA 1985 notices and the views of any Leasehold Valuation Tribunal on reasonableness.** Performance management contracts might also be relevant to managing agents in terms of the management of the service charge itself. This chapter covers:

- Value for money
- Setting performance standards
- Relative improvement contracts
- Procurement specialists

As buildings become more sophisticated, many landlords find themselves providing an increasing multiplicity of services. There is also a slow but inextricable move within the industry away from the traditional view of the 'landlord and tenant' relationship, which was often seen as intrinsically adversarial, towards a relationship that acknowledges the perspective of supplier and customer.

In the light of this move and the need for owners to be aware of and to positively respond to the financial pressures placed upon occupiers, there is a growing appreciation of and requirement to achieve and demonstrate value for money in the provision of services.

Sections 21–25 of the *Code of Practice for Service Charges in Commercial Property* states that:

21   Contractors and suppliers of services, including site management teams and managing agents will be required to perform according to written performance standards.

22   Performance will be regularly measured and reviewed against these defined performance standards. Best practice recognises, where appropriate, that a relevant proportion of their budgeted remuneration will be subject to achieving (or surpassing) the agreed standards and paid as an incentive when these standards are met.

23   The services provided will be beneficial and relevant to the needs of the property, its owner, its occupiers and their customers.

24   The aim is to achieve value for money and effective service rather than lowest price.

25   The levels and standards of service provided for each property will be different depending on the nature, type and complexity of the property. On occasion there will be additional services provided outside the service charge. Occupiers are entitled to expect similar transparency, accountability, etc, in these services. The code will apply to these as well.

Performance contracts are a contracting methodology designed to meet the specific needs set down by the user, and where achievement against set performance standards can be measured and reflected in the cost incurred for the level of service actually provided.

By specifying the standards to be achieved, rather than the process, the onus is upon the service provider, particularly in a competitive tendering situation, to ensure the most cost effect processes and procedures are employed in order to achieve the specific needs of the customer. In this way, value for money can be achieved by ensuring that the optimum price is obtained to meet the specific standard of service required.

18.1 Value for money

The emphasis of the Code of Practice and thus best industry practice is in achieving 'value for money'. This is usefully defined as:

'Paying no more for no less than is required'.

The first step to achieving value for money therefore is to know and understand what service is required, to what standard the service is to be provided, and when the services are required.

Traditionally, service contracts are based on a detailed specification that sets out what services are to be performed, how these services are to be performed, when, and how frequently. For example, a cleaning specification may detail what surfaces are to be cleaned, how the cleaning is to be carried out, how often, and at what times.

However, this may not always result in value for money being achieved. The person preparing the specification is often not an expert in the field of cleaning, security, etc. and therefore in attempting to prepare a detailed specification of **how** the service is to be provided, the essential elements of the appropriate quality standards and timing may be ignored.

Contractors will usually tender and price what they have been asked to and therefore where a contractor adheres rigidly to a detailed specification this may result in a higher or lower standard of cleaning than is actually required. The higher standard of cleaning may carry with it an unnecessarily high cost, while the lower standard may be achieved at a lower cost but will not meet the customer's requirements and expectations.

A detailed specification might also set down specific times when cleaning operations are to be carried out which may be inappropriate or impractical. A requirement for the mall areas of a large shopping centre to be swept every two hours might seem appropriate to ensure a high standard of cleaning. But sweeping the mall floors during peak trading periods might be physically impossible due to the volume of customers, and sweeping the floors two hours after the centre has first opened might simply be unnecessary.

18.2 Setting performance standards

There are various methods of setting performance standards, which will be dependent upon the asset type, the service provided, the needs of the customer, and the facilities to record and monitor the standards to be achieved, such as:

- establishing the periods during which an item of equipment must be in full operational order;
- a minimum specified standard of service is to be provided and maintained;
- limiting the number of faults allowed in a period; and
- setting specific response targets for attending to repairs, etc.

Once established and agreed the level of performance achieved must be measured and reviewed on a regular basis.

Remuneration for the delivery of the service would then be linked to the performance achieved against the target performance standards set. If performance falls below the agreed standard there would be a reduction in cost. Similarly, the remuneration might be increased in the event that target performance standards are exceeded.

However, as performance contracts become more common there has been a growing trend towards 'risk pricing'. Contractors are adding additional costs to tender prices so that, if they were to win the contract, the reduced cost for performing below the agreed standard would in reality equal the actual cost of providing the service. Rather than incurring a penalty for performing below standard, the 'risk 'pricing' would give the service provider a bonus for simply meeting expectations rather than for exceptional performance.

This can be avoided by tendering the contract on a more traditional basis at the same time to provide a benchmark comparison for services. However, this will usually involve the service provider in additional up-front costs in preparing two tender submissions and therefore this can only really be done for large properties where these additional tendering costs can be readily absorbed in the contract price and will be negated by cost savings.

18.3 Relative improvement contracts

An alternative solution to fixed performance contracts as above is to consider a relative improvement contract.

This type of contract methodology avoids fixed targets which then controls the service provider's future actions but encourages the service provider to deliver continuous performance improvement using their specialist knowledge, skills and judgement to adapt to changing conditions and requirements.

The contract would be tendered in the usual way based on a performance contract (a contract specification setting down the outcome required rather than the process).

The service provider would then be encouraged to suggest ways of performing the contract on an ongoing basis to achieve cost savings and/or improvement in appropriate standards in order to exceed the value for money equation.

The important aspect of a performance contract of this nature is that the service provider and customer share the financial savings agreed. In this way the service provider has a vested interest in achieving value for money which will ultimately be filtered through to the service charge and the tenants.

Savings identified by the service provider resulting in improvements in the effectiveness of the service provided would be shared. Therefore, a saving of £10 identified as a result of a change in the way which the service is provided would result in a reduction in the contract sum of £5 representing a reduced cost to the client of £5 and an increase in the contractor's profit of £5.

Conversely, if the service standards are set at an inappropriately low level, the service provider and customer would share equally in any increased costs incurred in achieving the required standards.

Advantages

The advantage to performance or relative improvement contracts is that the contract sum, in theory, reflects the actual costs of achieving the service standards required.

The service provider is encouraged to constantly look for ways to improve the service standards achieved by having a financial interest in the resultant savings achieved.

Performance management focuses on the needs of the business, individual and customer.

Performance contracts will clearly vary in style and content but where implemented successfully should drive continual improvement in the delivery of services. They provide flexibility in adapting to changing tenants' demands and expectations and encourage mutual trust and a sense of partnership between customer and service provider.

Disadvantages

Possibly an advantage when working properly, but a disadvantage at any other time, performance contracts require a degree of trust between the service provider and customer implicit to which is a good working relationship.

Performance contracts by their very nature require constant performance measurement which can often be time consuming. However, for larger properties particularly with an on-site management team, the need to manage the service providers performance in achieving the standards agreed need not be particularly onerous.

18.4 Procurement specialists

Clause 36 of the Code of Practice for *Service Charges in Commercial Property* states that:

> 'The owner will be entitled to use a procurement specialist to obtain these services so long as the purpose is to achieve greater value for money and cost effectiveness (the fees being declared and charged to the service charge)'.

Procurement specialists should therefore be used where appropriate to ensure that the contract specification fully meets the owner's and occupiers' requirements and also to monitor and analyse the service provider's performance.

Where the aim is to achieve greater value for money, the costs of engaging a procurement specialist would normally (and subject as always to the terms of the lease) constitute a legitimate service charge cost.

19

Commercialisation

This generally applies to the commercial sector but there may be occasions where it affects the residential field (for example phone masts on roofs and historic buildings used as film sets). This chapter includes:

- Examples of income to be retained by the owner
- Examples of income to be credited in full to the service charge
- Examples of grey areas where a clear stated policy is required
- Communication and transparency
- Treatment of income in the service charge accounts

Landlords will usually seek to optimise the income from their investment and in addition to rents collected in respect of occupational leases, the owner may also receive income from a wide variety of other sources such as public telephones, poster sites, advertising hoardings, etc.

Income received in addition to the rent paid under the occupational leases, usually referred to as non-core, miscellaneous or (in the case of shopping centres) mall income is also now more commonly referred to as 'commercialisation'.

Commercialisation is particularly common, but not exclusive, to retail schemes where the public have general access to the scheme and numerous opportunities exist for generating additional income through advertising hoardings, promotional space and various activities carried out on the mall areas.

Many tenants object to income generated from common parts being retained by the landlord when it is the tenants who pay for the cleaning, lighting and other costs associated with these areas.

The treatment of such income is a subject of considerable variance from property to property and owner to owner and dependant upon the nature of the additional income generated there is an issue as to whether the income should properly belong to the landlord solely or whether it is income generated from the services supplied to, for or on behalf of the tenants.

The Code of Practice for *Service Charges in Commercial Property* states that any income derived from the provision of a service or activity, the finance for which is included in the service charge, will be treated as a service charge credit.

It is the nature of the activity that will often give an indication as to whether it is the landlord or tenants who should receive the benefit of the income. Owners should clearly state their policy on how costs and income generated from services and activities are allocated. The guidance provided in the Code of Practice for *Service Charges in Commercial property* can be summarised as follows:

- if the item is not funded by the service charge and does not use any services, the income goes to the owner 100 per cent;
- if the item is funded by the service charge, the income is credited to the service charge; and
- if the item uses some of the services and/or needs support from the site team who are paid by the service charge, a contribution, in accordance with the policy, will be made to the service charge.'

19.1 Examples of income to be retained by the owner

The most obvious example would be the rental income received from the lettable space of the building. Other examples might be income generated from car parks, mobile phone masts, advertising, radio aerials, etc.

Notwithstanding the principles set out in the Code of Practice for the treatment of miscellaneous income, the Code also states that where there is a separate cost or profit centre that generates income for the owner, which is not credited to the service charge account, the costs associated with maintaining and running that cost centre will not be allocated to the service account. If staff or services that form part of the service charge are used then the cost/profit centre will be incorporated into the service charge matrix.

19.2 Examples of income to be credited in full to the service charge

Example 1: As part of the building services a landlord provides recycling bins and a cardboard compactor to facilitate the recycling of waste. Until recently, compacted cardboard could be sold for recycling and in some circumstances the income generated from the sale of cardboard could often exceed the total cost incurred for waste disposal. As the costs of managing and disposing of the waste would be a cost borne by the tenants as part of the service charge it would therefore not be unreasonable to expect any income generated as a direct result of the provision of the services i.e. an efficient system for the recycling of waste, to be used to offset and defray the costs of providing that service.

Notwithstanding that it now costs businesses to recycle waste and it is most unlikely that anyone would actually pay to remove waste such as cardboard; this is a relatively simple and straightforward example. But matters can become more complex when income is generated from areas or activities which are not so obviously or directly part of the building's services, and where the income generated can often be considerable.

Example 2: Advances in technology with the introduction, for instance of electronic poster displays can substantially increase the number of adverts exhibited at a single location. This has therefore increased the value of prominent sites and locations and many landlords, not unreasonably, prefer to take advantage of these increased revenue opportunities.

Another example is the increase in the number of posters and adverts introduced into such areas as public or common parts toilets. Avoiding the obvious references to benefits of a captive audience, these adverts can generate significant income. However, the public toilets of a shopping centre will usually fall within the definition of the common parts and the cost of maintaining, lighting and generally servicing the toilets would invariably fall as a cost to the service charge.

However, the introduction of the advertising may not involve an increased cost of maintaining and servicing the toilets, but the fact that these areas are maintained, usually to a high standard, at the tenants' expense, would be a significant factor for the media company in placing the posters in these locations. Therefore, it might be possible to argue that the income generated from the posters is only achieved as a direct result of the standard and quality of the toilets and that therefore the income should be credited to the service charge and against the costs of maintaining those standards.

19.3 Examples of grey areas where a clear stated policy is required

Matters become even more complex when, for instance in the case of a shopping centre, the income is received and generated from an activity which is more closely identifiable as a 'letting' of retail or quasi-retail space.

It is more often usual to see a variety of temporary stands, barrows or stalls, located on and along pedestrian malls. As these are usually temporary or removable, they might only be used at peak trading periods and will often be let under a temporary licence or tenancy at will arrangement. The landlord may therefore view these lettings in the same way as any letting of a shop unit (albeit temporary) and retain the licence fees charged as rental income.

However the main occupational leases would usually designate the pedestrian malls as common parts, with the liability for the payment of a proportion of the cost of cleaning lighting, maintenance and repair of these areas included under the service charge.

The Code of Practice for *Service Charges in Commercial Property* also states that, if the use of the space is of a permanent of semi-permanent nature (e.g. barrows or kiosks located within the malls) it would be permissible for the landlord to retain the income as rent, i.e. to treat the letting as any other permanent letting of the scheme, but only provided that the landlord similarly treated the barrow or kiosk as any other shop unit for the purposes of calculating the service charge.

The barrow or kiosk space should be included in the service charge apportionment matrix and bear a fair and reasonable proportion of the total service charge costs for the scheme. Whether the terms of the agreement requires the kiosk or barrow operator to actually pay a service charge is irrelevant but what is important is that the remaining tenants do not subsidise these lettings and the landlord bears the cost including void periods.

Rental values for kiosk and barrow units are often higher per square foot than values achievable on standard shop units. This tends to reflect the increased turnover relative to floor space and the reduced operational overheads. Where service charge apportionments are calculated by reference to floor area, it is sometimes difficult to calculate an appropriate or proper proportion of the service charge relative to such units. A mobile barrow may not actually have a floor area which is capable of being calculated in accordance with the *RICS Code of Measuring Practice* and the relatively small area of a kiosk unit may give rise to a disproportionately low percentage of the service charge which does not reflect the relative benefit and use of the services received by the kiosk.

Therefore, as an alternative to including these areas within the apportionment matrix, a sum should be credited to the service charge to reflect a fair and reasonable contribution towards the benefit of the services provided.

19.4 Communication and transparency

Landlords should clearly state their policy on how costs and income generated from services or activities are allocated and the Code of Practice requires that transparency should be demonstrated at all times.

19.5 Treatment of income in the service charge accounts

One aspect that does not seem to be universally applied is the point at which income is applied to the service charge. In many instances, income is credited against expenditure and the net figure shown in the service charge account. This will distort the true cost of the service, does not conform to the principles of ensuring transparency in the service charge accounts, and will often give rise to difficulties in the proper and accurate benchmarking of costs.

A further anomaly that can occur, particularly in cases where management fees are based as a percentage of the service charge expenditure, is that a large credit within the service charge would reduce the management fee due to the managing agents – in effect the managing agents are paying the tenants – when there might be considerable involvement in managing the accounts and in generating the income which is credited to the service charge.

While best practice requires that fees are on a cash basis rather than being calculated as a percentage of expenditure, income should be credited to the service charge after calculation of the management fee. In this way not only is the anomaly referred to above avoided, but the costs and income receipts are shown separately in the service charge account which is considered to be good accounting practice.

20

Marketing and promotions

This area generally concerns commercial property and covers:

- Marketing and promotions – a shared cost
- Best practice
- Consultation with tenants
- Sharing of information

Retail and leisure schemes in the UK are facing ever-increasing competitive pressures as a result of which many schemes have historically sought to attract and retain customers through the proactive marketing and promotion of the scheme as a retail destination.

In May 2004 a *Good Practice Guide for Shopping Centre Marketing and Promotions* was produced by the Property Managers Association (PMA) in consultation with and supported by various industry organisations which estimated that the UK Industry's annual spend in shopping centre marketing exceeded £80m per annum.

The *Good Practice Guide for Shopping Centre Marketing and Promotions* provides guidance in relation to the planning, formulation, consultation and success measurement of marketing and promotional planning.

The apportionment and recovery of expenditure in respect of marketing and promotions relating principally to shopping centres, as well as retail and leisure parks is a matter that gives rise to considerable debate and dispute. This chapter does not concern itself with how to organise marketing and promotion activities but deals with the circumstances where marketing and promotional expenditure is incurred and is to be included as a service charge cost.

20.1 Marketing and promotions – a shared cost

While all businesses, great and small, will to some extent carry out some marketing or advertising of their business, smaller or independent retailers will generally not have the financial wherewithal to mount a marketing campaign intended to reach a wider catchments audience through the use of more expensive media such as radio or TV advertising and would often be limited to simple local advertising.

In taking a lease in a modern shopping centre the small or independent retailer is able to take advantage of more effective and pro-active marketing and otherwise cost prohibitive media through the pooling of financial resources with the other retailers. The independent retailer can also benefit from the owner's ability to procure appropriate and cost effective marketing and promotional expertise.

Many large and national multiple retailers spend considerable sums each year in own brand marketing and (particularly in the case of major or anchor tenants for a scheme) will often be a significant draw for customers in their own right. Indeed, some household names have historically not generally been known to advertise – their name and mere presence in a scheme being sufficient in itself to attract customers. This is not the case today and due to increasing retail competition and narrowing margins nearly all major retailers will actively advertise and promote themselves in order to maintain market share.

These large or national multiple retailers will sometimes therefore object to the inclusion of marketing and promotional expenditure within the service charge where this is seen to conflict with or duplicate their own brand marketing. Furthermore, national multiple retail chains are often as concerned with overall market share as much as individual store performance and expenditure incurred in marketing and promoting a single location is often seen simply as a cost incurred in taking custom from another trading location (perhaps in the same or a neighbouring town) with no actual overall increase in total turnover for the business.

It is also frequently argued that the marketing and promotion of a retail and leisure scheme not only benefits the tenants but also the landlord.

A successful scheme that has an established customer base will lead to increased turnover and enhanced profits for tenants. This in turn might lead to increased rental income for the landlord at review or indeed a more immediate increase in income if the tenant's lease provides for rent to be paid each year as a percentage of turnover.

The potential for improved turnover and profit will increase demand for units within the scheme which will result in a reduction in landlord voids. All other things remaining equal, increased rental values and reduced voids would result in an increase in capital value of the landlord's asset.

Tenants will therefore often argue that it is reasonable for the landlord to bear a proportion of the marketing and promotional expenditure to reflect the benefit received in terms of increased rental and capital value.

20.2 Best practice

The RICS Code of Practice for *Service Charges in Commercial Property* states that the funding of marketing and promotional activities is recognised as a shared cost to be borne by both owners and occupiers in partnership.

In the case of older leases which do not specifically refer to marketing and promotions, landlords will often use a sweeper clause as authority to sustain that they have the ability to recover such costs through the service charge. The availability of the sweeper provision to recover such costs, not originally envisaged or in contemplation at the grant of the lease can be a source of conflict and much debate between the owner and occupiers.

However, it is the authors' experience that in such circumstances occupiers will often agree to the recovery of the cost of marketing and promotions under the provisions of a sweeper clause where the owner makes a significant contribution towards the costs in accordance with best practice principles.

Where a lease specifically provides for the recovery of the cost of marketing and promotions it is recommended that the amount of the contribution from the owner should be agreed during the negotiation stage and written into the lease. The contribution from the owner is reasonably and typically 50 per cent of the marketing expenditure.

20.3 Consultation with tenants

It should not automatically be assumed that marketing and promotion of a retail scheme is always desirable or necessary. A scheme that is dominant in a particular location, with no other direct competition may not require any costs to be incurred in marketing and promotions.

However it is not unusual for expenditure to be incurred simply because marketing and promotions is seen as an essential part of the services provided by landlords of retail schemes rather than because there is a clear need to pro-actively market the scheme.

It is therefore essential to initially establish if there is a need to market the centre.

In order to formulate an effective marketing and promotions strategy, it is recommended to conduct a SWOT analysis of the scheme (identifying strengths, weaknesses, opportunities and threats). It is also important to have up-to-date knowledge of competing centres and any other issues which might affect the trading potential for the scheme.

If there is a need for marketing, the marketing plan and strategy should be based on clear objectives and reflect the business and strategic goals for the scheme. These objectives should be specific and measurable and the marketing plan reviewed on a regular basis to assess whether the key outputs are being achieved.

The marketing plan should be prepared and communicated to tenants in advance and the service charge budgets (and actual statements of expenditure) should clearly state the gross expenditure and the contribution from the owner.

20.4 Sharing of information

Marketing and promotions should be regularly monitored and reviewed to analyse their effectiveness against the desired objectives and budget. In doing so, the owner or managing agents will often collect certain information and data essential for measuring the effectiveness of the marketing and promotion strategy, such as:

- customer footfall measurement;
- tenant trading/turnover index;
- dwell time measurement; and
- frequency of customer visits.

Any costs associated with the collation and analysis of this information would normally be included as part of the marketing and promotions budget and would fall as a cost to the service charge (with an appropriate contribution from the owner).

Since the service charge supports such expenditure, it is essential that such information is shared with retailers although the commercial sensitivity and confidentiality of any data supplied by retailers (e.g. sales/turnover data) should be respected at all times and used only for the purpose of measuring the effectiveness of the marketing plan.

21

Sunday trading

One of the few pieces of legislation to directly effect service charges in commercial property, and in particular the apportionment of service charge costs is the *Sunday Trading Act* 1994. This area is generally for commercial property and this section covers the following topics:

- The *Sunday Trading Act* 1994
- Keep open clauses in leases completed prior to 26 August 1994
- Keep open clauses in leases completed after 26 August 1994
- Service charge recovery for leases granted after 26 August 1994
- Service charge recovery for leases granted prior to 26 August 1994
- Sweeper clauses
- Recovery of Sunday trading costs

21.1 The *Sunday Trading Act* 1994

The Act, which modified the *Shops Act* 1950, came into effect on the 26th August 1994 and permits shops in England and Wales to trade seven days a week, subject to certain conditions. In particular it:

- allows retail units in excess of 3,000 ft^2 (internal area) to open for six consecutive hours between 10 a.m. and 6 p.m. on Sundays;
- allows small units (below 3,000 ft^2) to trade at any time on a Sunday; and
- exempts certain large shops from the six-hour trading guideline. These include farm shops, car and cycle

accessories retailers, off-licences, petrol stations as well as retail units in railway stations and motorway service stations.

The Act, for the most part, deals with the types of shops that may open and employees' rights. The only section that is particularly relevant to landlords is section 3 that provides:

'(1) Where any lease or agreement (however worded) entered into before the commencement of this section has the effect of requiring the occupier of a shop to keep open for the serving of retail customers:

(a)   during normal business hours, or

(b)   during hours to be determined otherwise than by or with consent of the occupier,

that lease or agreement shall not be regarded as requiring, or as enabling any person to require, the occupier to open the shop on Sunday for the serving of retail customers.

(2) Subsection (1) above shall not affect any lease or agreement -

(a)   to the extent that it relates specifically to Sunday and would (apart from this section) have the effect of requiring Sunday trading of a kind which before the commencement of this section would have been lawful by virtue of any provision of Part IV of the *Shops Act 1950*, or

(b)   to the extent that it is varied by agreement after the commencement of this section.'

21.2 Keep open clauses in leases completed prior to 26 August 1994

Shopping centre leases will usually stipulate hours during which a tenant is obliged to be open for trading (the keep open provisions) and other hours during which the tenant is permitted to trade (the permitted hours).

Where a lease was entered into before 26 August 1994 and contains a keep open provision (which may or may not be variable) the landlord cannot require a tenant to open on Sundays. If a tenant chooses not to open on Sundays, he or she cannot be held in breach of the lease.

However, if the landlord and tenant have agreed that the lease should be varied to include Sunday trading hours then it would be enforceable. It should also be noted that for this agreement or variation to the lease to be effective it must have taken place after 26 August 1994.

If a pre-26 August 1994 lease specifically stipulates that the premises will be open for Sunday trading then this would be enforceable. However, it would appear that in these circumstances, it would only be enforceable had Sunday trading been lawful prior to the enforcement of the Act (i.e. if it was lawful pursuant to Part IV of the *Shops Act* 1950).

21.3 Keep open clauses in leases completed after 26 August 1994

Leases granted after 26 August 1994 will not be covered by Section 3 of the *Sunday Trading Act* and the wording of the lease itself will need to be carefully checked to see if the definition of trading hours includes Sunday trading.

21.4 Service charge recovery for leases granted after 26 August 1994

Assuming the service charge provisions in the lease are drafted in wide enough terms to include Sunday trading, the landlord will be able to recover the service charges from the tenant even if he or she chooses not to open.

If the lease requires the tenant to keep open during Sunday trading hours and the tenant does not do so, then the tenant would be in breach of its lease. However, while the courts have been reluctant to force a tenant to trade notwithstanding the clear breach of the lease, there is no reason to believe that the courts would be reluctant to nevertheless force the tenant to pay its proportion of the service charge

The situation would be different if the lease did not provide for the tenant to keep open during Sunday trading hours. Although a tenant who is not required by the provisions of the lease to open at specific times, and chooses to close, for example, on a weekday, would probably be bound in any event to contribute to the services provided on the day it chooses to close, it is not certain that the courts would extend such an obligation to Sundays, unless the lease specifically provided for that. Although the *Sunday Trading Act* is silent as regards service charges, the general tone is to prevent an unwilling tenant from being obliged to open on Sundays and therefore it seems reasonable to expect the courts to take the view that if the tenant is not obliged to open on Sundays, then neither would it be obliged to contribute to the service charges.

21.5 Service charge recovery for leases granted prior to 26 August 1994

Section 3 of the *Sunday Trading Act* prevents a tenant being required to open even if its lease provided that it should open during 'normal business hours'. Derivations such as 'permitted', 'usual', etc. would not affect the situation.

It therefore follows that the landlord cannot require the tenant to pay the services incurred on Sundays, even if Sunday trading is regarded to be included within the generally accepted definition of 'normal business hours' unless the lease very specifically and categorically states as much.

However, the landlord and tenant can agree to vary the lease to include Sunday trading hours as referred to above and any agreement should include an undertaking on the part of the tenant to pay a proportion of the cost of providing the services.

21.6 Sweeper clauses

Sweeper clauses are designed to extend the heads of service charge rather than extend the period of time on which the services are provided.

In the absence of any specific reference to Sunday trading either within the main body of the lease or the service charge provisions, the existence of a 'sweeper provision' would not in itself be sufficient to enable the landlord to recover costs of Sunday opening through the service charge. For leases granted prior to or after 26 August 1994 it is unlikely that the courts will uphold that a sweeper clause permits the landlord to recover charges incurred on a Sunday if the lease clearly did not envisage such charges being recoverable from the tenant.

21.7 Recovery of Sunday trading costs

At one stage during the passage of the bill, it was proposed that the Act should contain a detailed schedule setting out how service charges should be apportioned in centres where some shops were open and others closed. This proposal was dropped and it is now a question of examining the wording of the service charge documentation to determine where liability lies.

It seems the only way that a landlord would be able to recover the costs of services incurred on a Sunday from those tenants who do open (and those that don't but whose leases provide for the recovery of such costs) is to separately calculate the Sunday trading costs and apportion the costs between the trading tenants. This will require the setting up of a separate service charge schedule and would be the only practical way of dealing with the situation, particularly where some of the tenants are on new leases which require them to pay the costs of Sunday trading whether they open or not, and where some tenants have the choice. This would remain the position while the centre has a mixture of pre- and post-26 August 1994 leases.

The provision, or more correctly the lack of provision within the *Sunday Trading Act* to provide clear guidance or direction with regard to the apportionment of service charge costs relating to Sunday trading, are in practice broadly ignored throughout the property industry. Increased costs incurred in opening retail schemes for Sunday trading are generally apportioned to all tenants irrespective of whether leases are granted prior to or after 26 August 1994 and whether tenants open for trading or not.

22

Management fees

Most, but certainly not all, leases provide for the landlord to recover the cost of administering the building and the service charge. Unfortunately however there are a significant number of older leases which do not allow for any recovery of management charges. This chapter includes:

- Methods of charging
- Calculation of management fees – including or excluding income
- Calculation of management fees – VAT elected or non-elected properties

In addition to management charges there are other specialist and professional fees which are often incurred. These include professional building surveyor's or architects' fees for the tendering and supervision of major works contracts and specialist fees for advice on such matters as health and safety or energy procurement, etc. While a lease may not allow for management fees it may well be possible to charge legitimately for some or all of these additional fees. This is especially the case if they form part of the costs of carrying out a function the cost of which can be recovered.

If you are used to commercial management you will find the rules attached to the residential sector impose a whole raft of requirements which need to be costed. In a similar vein the requirements of commercial management bring with them their own peculiar problems (e.g. VAT accounting and returns).

Unless the lease states to the contrary, the management fee is generally regarded as being the cost of the manager (including an element of reasonable profit) for managing the services comprised in the service charge. The 'manager' may be the landlord, a management company, or the landlord may appoint managing agents.

Typically these costs would include the supervision of the on-site team, overseeing the site contractors and the accounts work necessary to budget, forecast, manage, disperse, balance and apportion the service charge. Owners should also ensure that the management fee being charged to the service charge relates only to work carried out in managing the service charge and does not include the cost of other services provided by the managing agents for the benefit of the owner; or that the fees relate to matters between the owner and an individual occupier, e.g. enforcement of tenant covenant (including collection of rent), cost of letting units, providing landlord consents for assignments, subletting or alterations, rent reviews, etc.

It is common practice for management fees to be levied based on a percentage (often 10 per cent) of the cost of the services and in many cases both owners and occupiers are happy to accept this as a rough-and-ready approach. This is often reduced for larger properties in recognition of the fact that an increase in the cost of the front-line services does not necessarily result in a corresponding increase in the cost of managing the provision of the services.

Many fee scales are historic and bear little relation to the actual amount of work involved. Others are based on external factors and may or may not reflect a certain hope value of associated business. Some even reflect a desire to take on business and make a profit on selling it on rather than trading.

In a competitive market these factors cannot be ignored but it is very important that the fees charged should be sufficient to undertake the work required to a professional standard – It is very easy to quote 'the going rate' without considering exactly what is required.

This position has been re-affirmed by the recent case of *St. Modwen Developments (Edmonton) Ltd v Tesco Stores Ltd* [2006]. In this instance it was held that the landlord's right to charge a management fee was determined by the terms of the lease, as a matter of construction, and the landlord could only charge what it cost to manage the services and not a figure based on a proportion of expenditure, notwithstanding that this was common practice.

Indeed, for the commercial sector as more tasks are delegated to on-site management teams and with the increased use of facilities management companies (often introduced as a second tier of management to carry out some or many of the roles traditionally carried out by the managing agent in respect of the day-to-day management and supervision of services) management fees calculated as a percentage of actual expenditure are no longer considered appropriate and a disincentive to the delivery of value for money.

The RICS Code of Practice for *Service charges in Commercial Property* states that best practice requires that fees are on a cash basis rather than being calculated as a percentage of cost expended. Those responsible for setting such fees should ensure that the fee agreed reflects the reasonable price for work properly required in relation to the operation and management of the services and have due regard to the works necessary to achieve compliance with the Code of Practice.

It is often the case that a landlord will seek to charge a management fee where the lease specifies a maximum amount (e.g. ten per cent), while actually paying the managing agent substantially less thereby effectively making a profit from the supply of services.

Best practice requires that there will be transparency in the management fee charged and that the management service should be regularly tendered or benchmarked against the market.

Management fees charged to residential dwellings will be subject to the reasonableness tests set out in section 19 of the LTA 1985.

RICS publishes a number of draft management contracts and has recently revised the residential one. This gives a very firm basis on which to build your management fee. It has a standard set of functions which are included in the basic fee and then a further menu of additional services which can be provided at extra cost. The further services include dealing with major works, out of hours attendance at meetings, answering pre-contract enquiries, acting as company secretary, etc. (It really is amazing how meetings can be scheduled within office hours if the alternative would involve an extra charge!) Of course every case is different and you do not have to charge extras if you do not want to.

22.1 Methods of charging

The following methods of charging are used widely:

- fixed rates;
- percentage of total expenditure;
- performance related fees;
- landlord managed properties; and
- scale fees.

Fixed rates

In many ways this is a preferred method particularly for residential work as it sets out to reflect the actual costs involved. Many agents quote a basic per unit rate but this should, if it is used, be adapted to each building as clearly there are basic costs which will arise regardless of the size of the property. Remember that where apportionments vary the actual charge made to each unit will differ.

Consideration should be given to the actual costs involved in servicing the instruction which may lead to adopting a minimum fee according to the work involved. Clearly this will be much lower if no regular services are provided.

Involvement with a management company might also require consideration of what extra costs this may involve. The managing agent might not have anything to do with the company's affairs but the clients may need some help and be incapable of functioning without it.

When dealing with a management company, clear lines of communication and demarcation must be established at the outset.

The price for the management service should be fixed for a reasonable period (e.g. three years) and may be subject to indexing. However, care needs to be taken to ensure that the index is likely to reflect actual variations in the costs of providing the management service.

In order to cover set up costs it is common either to secure a contract to run for an extended period or to provide for a set-up fee. This could be payable at the outset or if the contract is prematurely curtailed. When dealing with residential property you could consider the effects of right to manage and the consultation requirements of section 20 of the LTA 1985 as amended.

Right to manage will enable 50 per cent of leaseholders who comply with the somewhat complicated rules to frustrate a contract.

Section 20 requires consultation in the statutory form if a contract is to run for more than a year and any lessee is paying more than £100 in a service charge period towards its costs.

If there is a recognised tenants association and they have served the appropriate notice they also have consultation rights.

Percentage of total expenditure

This method is more common in commercial management although the Code of Practice for *Service Charges in Commercial Property* sets out to do away with it. Such linkage is no longer regarded as appropriate and is usually seen as a disincentive to the delivery of value for money. The more effort the manager makes to keep costs down the less he or she is paid!

Even if the manager has done his or her job to the best of his or her ability they will still be open to criticism from tenants. It is far better to avoid that potential.

Fees based on a percentage of expenditure are common when dealing with the supervision and administration of major works as distinct from basic services in the residential sector.

It should nevertheless be noted that both commercial and residential leases frequently quote percentage-based management fees as the basis for calculating the service charge and in the absence of the ability to alter the terms of the lease the tenant's liabilities may, relatively speaking, be fixed.

Where leases cap or limit the amount of fees recoverable under the service charge the landlord/owner should bear the cost of any shortfall. The quality of the management service should not be compromised by what might be historic lease constraints in the recoverability of costs.

Performance related fees

These are far more common in the commercial sector although are not used extensively due to the problems in assessing performance criteria in order to calculate the fees actually due (see chapter 18 on performance management contracts).

Landlord managed properties

Care needs to be taken in referring to the lease to discover exactly what is allowed. Some leases make specific provision allowing the landlord to make a charge if he or she manages himself. This may be by a variety of means.

In other cases the lease may only provide for the recovery of costs directly incurred which may include the costs of employing a managing agent. Care should be taken to ensure that charges are recoverable. It may be appropriate to employ a managing agent if the landlord cannot recover his or her own time costs.

Scale fees

Occasionally some older leases make reference to the management fee being calculated in accordance with the scale fees laid down by the RICS.

However scale fees were abolished many years ago following comments made by the Monopolies and Mergers Commission to the effect that scale fees operated against the public interest.

In *Thames Side Properties Ltd v Brixton Estate plc.* (1997) it was held that in circumstances where the lease did not envisage abrogation of the scale fees and therefore made no reference to an alternative basis of calculation, the replacement should be calculated as the fee for managing the building which would be payable after arm's length negotiations between the landlord and a prospective managing agent.

22.2 Calculation of management fees – 'fees on fees'

Service Charge expenditure will often include fees and expenses paid to other professionals engaged from time to time in relation to specific projects or the provision of certain services. For instance: a building surveyor or architect might be employed to specify, tender and subsequently project manage and supervise a programme of major repair works.

However, where the lease is silent on the basis of calculation of the management fee but the management fee is nevertheless calculated as a percentage of the total service charge costs, a particular anomaly can arise which is often referred to, erroneously, as 'fees on fees'.

The problem can best be explained as illustrated below:

Cost of works	£100,000
BS fees @ 10%	£10,000
Total cost	£110,000
Management fee @ 10%	£11,000
Total service charge	**£121,000**

In the above example the building surveyor instructed in respect of the major repair works receives a fee of £10,000 whereas the property manager receives a fee of £11,000.

Some tenants would view the fee paid to the property manager as excessive on the basis that the property manager's involvement has been limited only to instructing the building surveyor/architect; whereas it is the building surveyor/architect that has been responsible for the actual work of preparing the specification, tendering and subsequently monitoring the works.

Furthermore, the total fees included in the service charge relating to the major repair contract would be considered excessive compared with usual market rates for the management of such projects.

Where the lease states that the management fee is to be calculated as a fixed percentage of the total expenditure the calculation as above would be in accordance with the terms of the lease even though the resultant total fees charged to the service charge might be considered excessive.

For residential properties this basis of charging has been affirmed by the Lands Tribunal. Even where the lease does not specify a fixed percentage, the property manager has additional obligations and duties beyond simply instructing the building surveyor/architect, i.e. in complying with statutory procedures (service of section 20 notices, etc.). In certain circumstances this basis of calculating the management fees may not give an unfair result particularly where the calculation produces a reasonable overall fee.

So far as commercial property is concerned, best practice suggested that the management fees should reflect the extent of the work required in managing and supervising the provision of the services.

If the lease specifies a management fee calculated as a specified percentage of total costs then, as above, the fee is correctly calculated in accordance with the terms of the lease.

Where the lease is silent, but the management fee is nevertheless calculated as a percentage of costs, the fee charged should only reflect the extent of the property manager's involvement in instructing and directing the building surveyor/architect. Accordingly the management fee should reasonably be calculated based on the building surveyor/architect's fee element only and should ignore the cost of the works themselves.

Cost of works	£100, 000
BS fees @ 10%	£10, 000
Total cost	£110, 000
Management fee @ 10% based on fee element only	£1, 000
Total service charge	**£111, 000**

In this example the total fee included in the service charge relating to the works of £11,000 reflects a cost more closely in line with reasonable market rates for work of this type.

Where management fees are calculated as a fixed sum, this anomaly does not arise.

22.3 Calculation of management fees – including or excluding income

The RICS Code of Practice for *Service Charges in Commercial Property* discourages management fees based on a percentage of expenditure. However where management fees are calculated on a percentage basis (i.e. in accordance with the terms of the lease) the fee should be calculated before any credit for income to the service charge is taken. If this is not done the managing agent will see his or her fee reduced below that which would be based on the expenditure which he or she has presided over. In an extreme theoretical case this would result in the managing agent paying to manage rather than being paid!

In many cases it is probably also appropriate to charge a fee for collecting income to be credited to the service charge other than by way of standard contribution especially if it involves collecting money from a third party.

22.4 Calculation of management fees – VAT elected or non-elected properties

One area which often causes problems, in relation to commercial properties, is the basis of calculation of the management fee when the property is non-elected for tax but where the lease specifies that the management fee is to be calculated at a fixed percentage of expenditure.

Example: The lease limits the management fees chargeable by the managing agents to ten per cent of the total service charge. The total service charge (excluding fees) is £80,000 exclusive of VAT.

Opted for tax

Where the property is elected, the management fee would be calculated as follows:

Service charge costs (ex. VAT)	£80,000
Management fee @ 10% (ex. VAT)	£8,000
Total service charge	£88,000

When invoicing the tenants, VAT would be added to the total service charge in the usual way. The total service charge (including VAT) would therefore amount to £103,400

Non-opted to tax

Where the property is NOT ELECTED the management fee is often mistakenly calculated at ten per cent of the total service charge cost (including VAT) with VAT then added to the management fee.

Service charge cost (inc VAT)	£94,000
Management fee @ 10%	£9,400
VAT on management fee @ 17.5 %	£1,645
Total service charge	£105,045

This problem only arises where the lease specifically states the management fee is to be calculated (i.e. capped) as a specified percentage of the total expenditure.

On the face of things this might seem to be a reasonable calculation as the fee is calculated at ten per cent of the service charge 'cost' which, as the building is non-elected is £14,000 greater than the 'cost' of an elected building. But, this assumes that payment of the managing agent's fees is the responsibility of the tenant – it is the owner who is responsible for payment of the management fees. Under the service charge arrangements the tenant's covenant to reimburse the landlord a proportion of the landlord's costs incurred in providing the services, which includes the cost for the management and administration of the service charge.

As the managing agent's fees are the responsibility of the landlord, they must be treated, for VAT purposes, in the same way as any other invoice for the supply of goods and services to the property.

The landlord cannot charge VAT on an exempt supply. If a property is exempt (i.e. an election to tax has not been made) the total management fees including VAT cannot exceed the amount stated in the lease (in this example 10%) of the aggregate of the other costs of providing the services, including VAT.

Therefore, in interpreting the operative provision of the lease, that the management fee is to be calculated based on 10 per cent of the service charge costs, the two must be viewed on the same basis either inclusive or exclusive of VAT.

The correct calculation is such circumstances would therefore be:

Service charge cost (inc. VAT)	£ 94,000
Management fee @ 10% (inc. VAT)	£ 9,400
Total service charge	£103,400

This basis of calculation gives the same management fee in either instance which in the circumstances must be the correct result. Alternatively, and using the example above, the managing agent would be £1,400 better off managing the building on a non-elected basis, where managing the VAT is far simpler. Another way of looking at it is the managing agent incurs a reduction in his or her fee simply because the landlord opts to tax – notwithstanding the elected property would involve the agent in greater work. Clearly this makes no sense but the veracity with which the alternative case is often put must beg the question as to whether such situations are viewed by a small minority as a 'trick of the trade' to obtain inappropriately increased fees.

23

Change of owner or managing agents

When properties are sold the new owners will often want their preferred managing agent to manage their new acquisition. There will also be circumstances which might determine that a change of managing agent is appropriate, but it is not a course of action which should be embarked upon without a great deal of consideration. Management knowledge is a very valuable thing and may generate considerable cost savings. As an example an agent who knows the foibles of a communal heating system may be able to save unnecessary costs dealing with it.

Whether as a result of a change in ownership or as a result of a transfer of responsibility between agents without a sale it will be necessary to organise the transition in as smooth a way as possible. Timing should be considered to fit in with the service charge year and it may be desirable to consider paying both the old and new agents for an overlap period. Owners should consider accounting costs relating to this.

However, considerable problems can be experienced following a change of ownership and/or managing agents.

Often the problems stem from delays and sometimes reluctance on the part of the previous managing agent to supply details of expenditure incurred during the period of their tenure to the new managing agents. This invariably results in what can often be significant delays in reconciling accounts, etc. The problem is exacerbated by the different account codes and descriptions used by different landlords and managing agents.

Guidance for commercial property

In an effort to resolve these problems and to present the industry generally in a far more favourable light, the Code of Practice for *Service Charges in Commercial Property* gives clear guidance as to best practice following a change of ownership and/or managing agents as follows:

> **'56** The budget will be issued in such a way that it provides sufficient information to enable occupiers to compare it with the last issued certified accounts. Details of how swiftly accounts will be closed and handed over will be made available at completion. Where the owner or managing agent was not responsible for the earlier years, they will convert the data into a consistent format for comparison.

> **57** As soon as practicable, but not later than four months, following the date of completion of a sale of a property, the seller will provide the buyer with full details of all service charge expenditure, accruals, pre-payments etc for all outstanding service charge years up to the date of sale.'

Significantly there is a responsibility for owners in this process.

When dealing with a change of ownership the buyer should ensure that the sale contract places the seller under a positive obligation to provide details relating to the service charge expenditure relating to the period(s) of ownership. Depending upon the timing of the sale in relation to the service charge accounting period the seller/previous managing agents is to provide either:

- a full service charge disclosure; or
- a service charge income and expenditure reconciliation should be provided.

For its part the seller should expect, as a cost of disposal of the asset, to continue to remunerate the incumbent managing agents where they are required to effectively continue to administer the service charge for a temporary period post-sale.

Similarly, when appointing managing agents, owners and agents should seek to ensure that the contract between them includes provision for an 'exit strategy' in the event of sale or dis-instruction and for the managing agent to be contractually bound but continuing to be remunerated for the continued administration of the service charge and in passing all reasonable and requisite information to their successors.

Where a service charge income and expenditure reconciliation is required

Within one month of the date of completion, the seller/previous agent is to provide for the service charge accounting period from the current year start date to the date of completion:

- statement of service charge income, together with copies of tenant demands for on-account charges;
- statement of service charge expenditure, together with copies of paid invoices;
- back-up for period-start accruals and prepayments;
- service charge apportionment methodology;
- direct-charge methodology;
- reconciliation of direct-charges;
- reconciliation of landlord liabilities;
- service charge cash reconciliation;
- notes to accounts explaining level of expenditure, variances, etc.; and
- a detailed statement of arrears including information regarding bad debts, disputes and payment plans.

Where full service charge closure is required

Within four months of the date of completion, the seller is to provide for the service charge accounting period from the current year start date to the date of completion:

- back-up for period-end accruals and prepayments;
- statement of service charge income;
- statement of service charge expenditure;
- service charge apportionment methodology;
- direct-charge methodology;
- statement showing calculation of balancing service charges;
- reconciliation of direct-charges;
- reconciliation of landlord liabilities;
- notes to accounts explaining level of expenditure, variances etc.; and

- a detailed statement of arrears including information regarding bad debts, disputes and payment plans.

Where sinking funds or reserve funds exist

Where the seller operates sinking funds or, reserve funds the following information should be provided to the purchaser at least two weeks prior to the date of completion:

- a detailed listing the assets covered by the fund;
- a statement showing how the value of contributions to the fund have been assessed and allocated between the landlord and tenants;
- details of when the fund due to expire (i.e. the projected life expiry of the assets covered by the fund);
- details of the trust status of the fund;
- details of the fund's tax liability status;
- statement of fund value;
- fund transaction listing;
- fund contribution summary;
- notes to expenditure;
- interest summary; and
- tax summary.

The seller should transfer to the purchaser on the date of completion an amount equivalent to the fund value at the date of completion, allowing for interest accrued and all other transactional activity up to the date of completion. This should be accompanied by an updated statement of fund value and transactional listing.

Residential statutory trusts

In the residential sector all service charges and reserve funds are held under statutory trusts and the new owner will become the new trustee. Bad debts should not normally form part of residential service charge expenditure as they are generally recoverable against a lessee or his successor. If for whatever reason they are not the debt may well have to be made good by the vendor.

As regards reserve or sinking funds, these will run with the building. They cannot be refunded to either landlord or tenant and will need to be dealt with accordingly.

214

You should ensure that funds are transferred to appropriate accounts and be ready to provide statutory information on them.

Transfer of records

If you are giving up management of a property you should promptly pass on all details and records to the new agent. You should also consider the need to ensure that you keep copies of all your records in case there is a future dispute. In any event if you do not do so you should seek an undertaking from the new agent to give access to the files and if this is not forthcoming then you should consider retaining copies. You must retain copies of files required to comply with RICS, FSA government or other regulating authority.

You should ensure that the records which you pass on are accurate and that the accounts balance.

All information required to make demands and account for monies should be passed on promptly.

If you do not comply with the above you should expect in general to bear any additional costs resulting from your non-compliance.

24

Leasehold Valuation Tribunal

This section applies to residential property although Leasehold Valuation Tribunal decisions may well affect mixed developments. This chapter will cover:

- History and where we are today
- Advocate or expert?
- Merits of representing the client
- Reasonableness of service charges
- Amendment of leases
- Use of Lease amendment powers
- Applications in advance
- Management orders
- How to use the tribunal to avoid problems
- Emergency applications
- The costs issue
- Appeals – the Lands Tribunal
- Appearing at the LVT

24.1 History and where we are today

When Leasehold Valuation Tribunals were first established, it was on the basis that the Rent Assessment Committee sat as a Leasehold Valuation Tribunal. The make up of these committees was generally a lawyer, a chartered surveyor and a lay-member. Each committee had to have a chartered surveyor sitting on it but he or she could be out voted by the other members.

Over the years the system has been refined and it is now not uncommon to have two chartered surveyors or two lawyers sitting on a tribunal. There is a worrying development in that while leaseholders appear able to sit on the tribunal, chartered surveyors acting for landlords in the area concerned are not. This policy has been justified on the grounds of conflicts of interest but the downside is that the chartered surveyors on the panel may lack the necessary local knowledge and experience which would otherwise be invaluable.

With the implementation of the *Housing Act* 2004 the remit of the tribunals has been greatly increased as they now deal with many other matters involving property and have been rebranded as the Residential Property Tribunal Service. In effect all three titles still apply to the same service in some form or another and they appear both in statute and in communications, which can be confusing for those who do not appreciate the situation.

The fee structure also varies according to function, type of claim, value of claim and means of claimant. The maximum fee including the hearing fee is £500 but there is a complicated sliding scale for fees designed to enable those with very limited means or small claims to pay relatively little. While of laudable intent this may lead to a claim being brought which will cost far more than it is worth to defend (but that is a problem with our justice system).

An attempt is made to mitigate the costs problem by limiting the costs which the Leasehold Valuation Tribunal may award to £500 plus its fees. It will generally only award costs where the conduct of the parties justifies it and certainly not as a general rule.

24.2 Advocate or expert?

As chartered surveyors you are able to appear before the Leasehold Valuation Tribunal both as advocate and expert. If you appear as expert you are bound by the RICS practice statement on *Surveyors Acting as Expert Witnesses* and must attach the required declaration to any statement or proof of evidence. The statement requires that your first duty as an expert is to the tribunal and not to your client. Expert evidence must be your professional opinion untainted by the interests of your client. You must be fully aware of the contents of the statement before acting as an expert and provide a copy to your client in the circumstances outlined in the statement.

You should acquaint yourself with any RICS guidance on acting as an advocate or expert witness before an application is made.

If you act as both advocate and expert then you must make it clear when you are acting as an expert and when you are acting as an advocate.

In order to help with this you must consider what your true professional opinion is and what is open to argument. If you advance an expert opinion it must not be coloured to reflect your client's interest. That does not stop you from giving an expert opinion of why you believe an argument is incorrect provided that it is your unbiased expert opinion.

Virtually every case will be different and some will simply involve situations where the decision of the Leasehold Valuation Tribunal only matters to the client in so far as it confirms the direction which must be taken in order to ensure that costs are recoverable.

You may also consider whether or not you wish to be in a situation where your professional opinion is at odds with the case which you are advocating before a tribunal. It may help you to consider the fact that lawyer advocates are paid to advance a case in the best way in which they can, not to give the court their professional opinion on its merits. Explaining what you have done and why you have done it or want to do it is not the same.

24.3 Merits of representing the client

The tribunal system is intended to provide a cheaper alternative to the courts which also reflects its own expert opinion. It enables chartered surveyors to represent their clients rather than employing a lawyer to do so. The system is supposed to be an informal one although with its directions and documentation requirements it increasingly mirrors the courts. On the down side, inadequate pre-trial review can lead to wasted time producing evidence to refute heads of claim which should have been dismissed at an early stage.

One has to admit that having to produce paginated 'trial bundles' does lead to a greater understanding of the costs and work involved in litigation.

So long as you can avoid becoming over irritated by the proceedings you are likely to find the experience rewarding provided that you are comfortable presenting a case and summing it up, and can react to circumstances as the hearing proceeds. You will need to ensure that the other side's case is properly cross-examined and that you possess the necessary knowledge and experience to do so.

Representing your client will avoid the need to instruct lawyers and to explain to them the complicated merits of the case. On the other hand by doing this you will not benefit from their advice. One of the most positive benefits is avoiding the possibility of your advocate following red herrings or failing to ask the obvious (to you) question which comes from your intimate knowledge of the case. You should also be able to react to questions as the hearing continues and retain far more control over its progress.

In the pre-hearing period you will usually take full control of the case unless this is undertaken by someone else which will avoid the need to liaise with your clients' solicitors – in which case you will need to undertake the work but retain a far greater control over it. The benefits of this will vary according to the working relationships you have with the lawyers.

You may feel that you would still benefit from some legal advice and if so you should seriously consider taking it. In certain cases you may even wish to call a lawyer as an expert witness.

Clearly the value of the case will have a great bearing on exactly who represents the parties but given the costs implications this is a field in which competent chartered surveyors are likely to play an increasing role.

24.4 Reasonableness of service charges

At the centre of the legislation regarding residential service charges is the proviso that, whatever the lease may say, the charges must be reasonable. The Leasehold Valuation Tribunal has power to decide both in advance and after the event whether or not a service charge is reasonable.

Before any action for non-payment of service charge involving forfeiture of residential property is taken, unless the debt has been admitted or determined by agreed post dispute arbitration, it must be determined by a Leasehold Valuation Tribunal.

It is important to note that the arbitration procedure appears to have been put into the legislation to encourage alternative dispute resolution as it is distinct from any procedure provided for within the lease. If you do follow the lease procedure then it appears that you will still have to go to the Leasehold Valuation Tribunal before obtaining forfeiture although the tribunal **may** of course endorse the result of the lease procedure!

It cannot be over emphasised that the Leasehold Valuation Tribunal decides upon whether or not the charges are **reasonable** – that does not mean that they will decide that anything other than the cheapest is unreasonable. It does mean that if you do not use the cheapest method you may need to justify your actions. On the other hand if you do use the cheapest and it is unsatisfactory the costs involved may well be unreasonable for the work undertaken.

The effect of this should be that you consider expenditure in each case on its merits. Asking the question: 'If I was paying for this myself, What would I do?' is always a good starting point, but you will also need to consider the other circumstances of the case.

One Leasehold Valuation Tribunal was willing to rule that the replacement of double glazing which had an extremely long cost recovery period was a reasonable expense.

Clearly one must take into account ongoing costs and it may well be reasonable to incur expenditure to save future costs particularly where equipment, such as scaffolding, is involved. If you are in doubt an advance application may be a wise precaution.

Unfortunately as Leasehold Valuation Tribunal decisions do not carry precedence caution must be taken in relying on a previous case and as is often the case circumstances may differ from the situation with which you are dealing.

24.5 Amendment of leases

The Leasehold Valuation Tribunal now has certain powers to amend leases. See section 162 of the CLRA 2002 which amends section 35 of the LTA 1987. Also section 163 which transfers jurisdiction from the court to the Leasehold Valuation Tribunal.

Under the 1987 Act a party to a lease could make an application to vary a lease because it failed to make satisfactory provision on certain grounds:

The following summarise the heads of claim but you should read the legislation in detail:

- repair or maintenance of the flat, building or grounds;
- insurance;
- repair or maintenance of installations;
- provision of services;
- recovery by one party from another party of expenditure that benefited the other party;
- the computation of the service charges; and
- the 2002 Act adds interest payable in default.

Safety and security and the condition of the common parts are to be taken into account. A service charge recovery above or below 100 per cent would be relevant.

Under section 36 of the LTA 1987 a respondent to a section 35 application may make an application to vary other leases in the event that the section 35 application is successful.

Under section 37 the majority of parties may make an application to vary all leases as long as the majority is a substantial one. The application must be made in respect of two or more leases and must be one which can only be achieved by varying all the leases.

The application may be made by the landlord or any of the tenants but only:

- if there are less than nine leases all or all but one of the parties must consent; and
- if there are more than eight leases less than 10 per cent may object and 75 per cent must consent.

The parties amount to one vote per lease and the landlord is not counted.

Sections 28 and 39, as amended, set out the orders which can be made.

24.6 Use of lease amendment powers

Clearly this is a wide ranging field but as the Leasehold Valuation Tribunal has the power to amend all leases with consent it is certainly worth considering an application as an alternative to deeds of variation.

If a matter is contentious or may involve increased burdens it may not be appropriate but if, for example, a management company has been struck off, an application for a variation to the Leasehold Valuation Tribunal to include a new company in the terms of all the leases may be more cost effective than the alternatives. The tribunal can make an order to amend all the titles at the land registry.

Clearly the greater the number of flats involved the more attractive a Leasehold Valuation Tribunal order becomes.

You should consider this route as a cost effective alternative where lessees are all in agreement.

Examples of defects to consider include:

- individual insurances;
- no power to collect a reserve fund;
- no power to collect service charge in advance;
- no provision to provide new services;
- abolition of outdated services;
- no power to pay a professional managing agent;
- split external decoration;
- responsibility to decorate rather than replace fittings which would be more cost effectively replaced; and
- redundant uses of common parts specified within leases.

The above list is far from exhaustive and items included within it may not be considered by a Leasehold Valuation Tribunal to be lease defects; never the less it provides a few suggestions of how this power can be used for the general benefit of all the parties involved.

24.7 Applications in advance

Given that the Leasehold Valuation Tribunal has the power to determine that expenditure is not reasonable after the event, with potentially serious cost implications for the Landlord, it must be seen as fair that this uncertainty can be addressed by an application to determine reasonableness in advance.

This course may well be appropriate where there is disagreement amongst the lessees as to what should be done. It may also be used to ensure that sufficient funds are forthcoming.

Unfortunately the protection given to lessees to avoid threats of forfeiture when unreasonable demands are made is often used to delay payment of reasonable demands. In the past the threat of action would prompt mortgagees to pay service charges but nowadays it is just as likely to elicit a response based on lessee rights to avoid forfeiture and a refusal to pay as a result of them.

This type of refusal is often accompanied by what you may see as unreasonable requests to give notice of your future actions. You may consider a response indicating that you have given them notice of default and give no further undertaking to provide any further notice of action. On the other hand if you have obtained a judgement for the service charges due or a predetermination of the reasonableness of the charges from the Leasehold Valuation Tribunal the mortgagee's security will be at potential threat.

It can therefore be seen that the predetermination not only secures the landlord's peace of mind but can also speed up cash flow as reference to the Leasehold Valuation Tribunal has already been made in respect of the works covered by it.

One final further advantage is that by involving the Leasehold Valuation Tribunal in reaching an independent decision which may be unpopular with any party, the relationship between all the parties may be preserved.

24.8 Management orders

Under sections 21–24 of the LTA 1987 a lessee may apply to a Leasehold Valuation Tribunal for a management order.

The procedure for this is set down within the Act and management orders under this provision must be made as a result of shortcomings in the existing management.

You would be forgiven for assuming that the new right to manage under the CLRA 2002 would supersede these provisions but this is not always the case.

Proceedings under this head can be taken by any lessee and may therefore be appropriate where some lessees do not wish to be involved in the costs of a right to manage order. On the other hand the failure in management may not affect the majority.

If for example the lessee on the top floor is suffering from a leaking roof, those below may not be concerned or may even be unwilling to contribute to the repair.

There is often a mistaken belief amongst leaseholders that the majority can override the legitimate rights of the minority. In such cases it may be necessary as a last resort to apply for a management order against a right to manage company or a lessee owned management company. (The two are not necessarily the same thing!) When the right to manage legislation was brought in this situation was appreciated and such an action was envisaged.

While accepting a Leasehold Valuation Tribunal management appointment may fit in well with your business plan, you should take care to ensure that you know what you are letting yourself in for. Every situation will be different but if the management failure has come about partly as a result of disputes between tenants or a failure to pay service charges, the job may be far from simple.

By the time the management order application is made it may be appropriate to make an order but in some cases the situation has resulted from problems which will not disappear with your appointment. It is important that you use the same considerations in accepting an appointment as you would when considering a new management – if you are not sure that you can make it work then you should not accept.

24.9 How to use the tribunal to avoid problems

This topic is covered above in greater detail. At the end of the day the Leasehold Valuation Tribunal is there to resolve disputes and give determinations both before and after the event. If it looks as if there is a serious dispute over the scope or form of works or the employment of contractors, you may make an application for a determination in advance of what will be a reasonable course of action.

Provided that there are no serious time constraints, a simple application may be the way forward.

If the Leasehold Valuation Tribunal has determined a course of action you should be able to rely upon the decision should your actions be challenged.

In an emergency where section 20 of the LTA 1985 expenditure limits would be exceeded an emergency application should be made to preserve your position.

24.10 Emergency applications

As the law has imposed limits on recoveries without going through section 20 of the LTA 1985 expenditure procedures, it is necessary to make an emergency application to the tribunal if you need to exceed the limits and do not have time to serve the notice and wait for the consultation procedures to run their course.

It is also necessary to make such an application if during a works programme additional works not covered within the expenditure limits become necessary or expedient. Works may become expedient, for example, if scaffolding is in place and they can be completed while it is there at a significant cost saving.

Unfortunately at the lower end of the scale the expenditure limit has been reduced significantly while the costs of health and safety requirements have risen. In many cases the costs of relatively small roof repairs may come within the limits not least because of scaffolding costs.

It is ironic that where large developments are concerned the expenditure limits have increased by up to 500 per cent whereas where only two flats are involved they have been cut by at least 50 per cent – This comes about by the removal of the £1000 de minimis limit.

Finally you should also note that there has been a subtle change to the wording of section 20 with the removal of the emergency provisions for commencement of work after notices had been served. The effect of this is that to be certain of recovery, you must make an emergency application even if you are dealing with an emergency that clearly should not wait.

It appears clear that an emergency application must be preferable to the prospect of litigation to establish a right to recover – even in a situation where emergency works were unavoidable and clearly in the interests of all parties yet no notices had run their course.

24.11 The costs issue

The costs which the LVT may award are limited to £500 plus its fees. Costs will generally only be awarded where the conduct of the parties justifies it and certainly not as a general rule.

The application and hearing fee structure varies according to function, type of claim, value of claim and means of claimant. The maximum fee including the hearing fee is £500 but there is a complicated sliding scale where fees are charged designed to enable those with very limited means or small claims to pay relatively little. While of laudable intent this may lead to a claim being brought which will cost far more than it is worth to defend but unfortunately that is a problem with our justice system and to be fair a satisfactory solution is evasive.

Under section 20C of the LTA 1985 an order may be made by the Leasehold Valuation Tribunal preventing costs involved in an action from being recovered from a service charge. Such an order is at the discretion of the tribunal. Recently an attempt was made by a losing party to argue that it would not be liable for its share of these costs through the service charge as the costs of Leasehold Valuation Tribunal proceedings are limited – in effect that would have made all lessees other than those bringing the unsuccessful action liable for the costs. The court found that this would have been unfair and ordered that the costs were a service charge expense.

On reflection the result in the above case meant that the lessees generally bore the not inconsequential costs of an unsuccessful action by individual lessees. The potential loss to the landlord meant that the action had to be rigorously defended. In this case the risk borne by the unsuccessful claimants was not proportionate to that of the landlords or the service charge generally.

24.12 Appeals – the lands tribunal

The appeal from the Leasehold Valuation Tribunal lies with the lands tribunal.

There are some important matters to note:

- application for leave to appeal must first be made to the Leasehold Valuation Tribunal within a strict time limit;
- if granted the appeal must be made to the lands tribunal (again within a strict time limit);
- if not granted an appeal against refusal may be made to the lands tribunal direct within a strict time limit of the refusal; and
- an application for leave to appeal to the lands tribunal out of time may also be made to the lands tribunal.

An appeal to the lands tribunal must be made on the form obtainable from the lands tribunal offices. The requirement to use the lands tribunal forms may not be clear in the Leasehold Valuation Tribunal documentation. Given the 28 day time limit, it would be wise to obtain these in advance.

Details of practice and procedure at the lands tribunal can be obtained from the lands tribunal. The notes are well worth reading to improve your professional knowledge generally.

In certain circumstances a chartered surveyor can bring an appeal on his or her client's behalf and with leave represent his or her client at the hearing.

There are three types of appeal procedure (written representations, informal hearing and formal hearing) the simplest of which may be particularly attractive to chartered surveyors.

If a chartered surveyor is to lodge an appeal on his or her client's behalf he or she will need to include a signed authority to do so from the client with the application.

The chartered surveyor will lodge the appeal on behalf of the client in his or her own name rather than his or her firm.

24.13 Appearing at the LVT

The following is intended to provide a few helpful pointers rather than an exhaustive instruction on how to conduct a hearing.

You need to be calm, well prepared and ready to listen before jumping in. You also need to be aware of the fact that the tribunal is largely made up of fellow professionals who may well be as nervous as you are.

The tribunal is not a court and is supposed to be informal but do not be surprised if the chairman attempts to conduct proceedings as if he or she were sitting as a judge. In fairness this may be to an extent necessary to prevent the proceedings getting out of control. Mercifully, I think sometimes, he or she does not have the powers of a judge with regard to commitment for contempt. The job description requires them to be polite and courteous at all times.

You should always treat the tribunal with respect and if you inadvertently mislead them you should bring this to their attention at the earliest opportunity.

Now that the tribunal's remit has been extended you should never rely upon their having direct detailed knowledge of the subject under discussion. There is a tremendous amount of knowledge and experience among the members of the tribunals but it would be unwise to assume that they were all fully conversant on every matter which was in dispute.

On the other hand you also need to be prepared to discover that they know far more than you do about a subject.

It is advisable to have prepared a proof of evidence which you can give to the other side and to each member of the tribunal – they can make notes on it as you expand your argument. It should have your name, qualifications and other relevant details, experience, etc. on it to avoid the need for them to be taken down by the tribunal (this also avoids errors with spellings, etc. on the written judgement). You may feel that your own copy would benefit from a large or bold font to help you deliver your case.

The proof will also assist the tribunal when discussing the judgement as they will have a written note of the salient points to which to add their own. It should also help to avoid confusion over what you actually said. A proof of evidence should not be considered as written evidence but as a record of your aural evidence. It should never the less make reference to the RICS *Surveyors Acting as an Expert Witness* practice statement if appropriate.

If you are to cross examine on an expert witness report or some other report which has already been presented you would also be wise to prepare your questions in advance. This can of course be done in a similar form to the proof although your questioning may alter as a result of the answers which you receive – you should be prepared to adapt.

While you may not anticipate some events you should try not to let them distract you. Be prepared to analyse the full implications of information which comes to light and not simply jump to a conclusion without thinking things through fully.

If you need to concede a point, fair enough but do think first before jumping to the wrong conclusion or accepting that you have done something wrong when in fact you have not.

As you conduct more hearings you should become more comfortable but be prepared to experience very different styles and levels of expertise. It is worth reflecting that the tribunal members will probably also refine their approach with experience! Don't be surprised to receive an unexpected question and be prepared to fill in the tribunal's knowledge (or that of your opposite number) quoting case law if necessary.

If you are to rely on complicated cases it may be worth while providing highlighted transcripts for the tribunal members to refresh their memories but do not forget a copy for the other side. In many cases these may be included in the trial bundle if there is one.

When a bundle has to be prepared by the other side make sure that they are clear on what you want included. If they are disputing inclusions of open documents, it may be necessary to provide these direct to the Tribunal. This should not be necessary but it is not unheard of.

Finally a word of warning on venues: The Residential Property Tribunal Service attempts to secure venues close to the subject property or convenient to the parties. Unfortunately this may cause problems with poor acoustics or bad lighting. If your eyesight is not perfect or you have hearing problems you should make this clear at the outset when the hearing is being arranged – if you cannot read your papers easily it is likely to be far more stressful putting your case.

25

Residential tenant's right to a management audit

Sadly there are relatively few areas, other than this one, in which chartered surveyors are given specific responsibilities by Parliament.

When carrying out one of these audits do not forget the specific rights of lessees to inspect insurance documentation and if you see fit include that area in your notice. If the landlord objects to disclosure you may wish to point out his or her legal obligations regarding disclosure to the tenants under notice which would make any refusal prima facie unreasonable.

Under Chapter V (Sections 76-84) of the *Leasehold Reform Housing and Urban Development Act* 1993 the right is to have an audit of the landlord's management of the relevant premises and appurtenant land carried out.

This chapter discusses:

- To what does the right apply?
- Who can exercise this right?
- Who is a qualifying tenant?
- What is the audit? – The importance of the RICS Management Code
- Who can carry out a management audit?
- What rights does the auditor possess?
- How is the right exercised?
- What happens once the notice is served?
- What happens if there is a superior landlord?
- What happens if the landlord disposes of his or her interest while the notice is current?

25.1 To what does the right apply?

The residential tenant's right to a management audit applies to residential premises containing two or more dwellings let by the same landlord.

25.2 Who can exercise this right?

In the case of a building consisting of two dwellings either or both qualifying tenants can exercise the right, but in the case of a building consisting of three or more dwellings not less than two thirds of the qualifying tenants are needed.

In the case of a single qualifying tenant the tenant can exercise the right.

25.3 Who is a qualifying tenant?

The qualifying tenant is a tenant of a long lease who pays common service charges.

There can only be one qualifying tenant per dwelling and the lessee who holds the shortest long lease on a dwelling will be the qualifying tenant. A person can be a qualifying tenant of more than one dwelling if held on a separate lease.

25.4 What is the audit? – The importance of the RICS Management Code

The audit is carried out to ascertain the extent to which the obligations of the landlord to the qualifying tenants with regard to management functions are being discharged in an efficient and effective manner.

In determining whether or not the obligations are being discharged in an efficient and effective manner under section 78(2) of the *Leasehold Reform, Housing and Urban Development Act* 1993: regard shall be had to any applicable provisions of any code of practice for the time being approved by the secretary of state under section 87.

The RICS *Service Charge Residential Management Code* has been approved by the Secretaries of State for England and

Wales under the terms of Section 87 of the *Leasehold Reform, Housing and Urban Development Act* 1993. The Code applies to properties where a service charge that varies according to the expenditure is payable, and the Landlord is not a public sector authority or registered housing association.

In addition there are further approved codes covering retirement housing published by the Association of Retirement Housing Managers and the RICS *Rent Only Residential Management Code* to cover rent only properties where service charges do not apply.

25.5 Who can carry out a management audit?

Subject to disqualifications contained in the Act:

- an accountant who is a registered auditor;
- a chartered surveyor; or
- any other qualified surveyor prescribed under regulations made by the Secretary of State.

can carry out a management audit.

The auditor may appoint such assistants as he or she thinks fit.

25.6 What rights does the auditor possess?

The auditor possesses the rights to:

- require Sect 21 LTA 1985 accounts;
- inspect supporting documentation as per sect 22 LTA 1985;
- require facilities to inspect and take copies of any other documents which he or she reasonably requires; and
- inspect the common parts.

It should be noted that the right to inspect documents goes beyond the section 22 rights to any document which the auditor reasonably requires.

25.7 How is the right exercised?

The right is exercised by notice under section 80 of the *Leasehold Reform Housing and Urban Development Act* 1993.

The notice must be given by the auditor to the landlord and signed by the tenants on whose behalf it is given. It must contain:

- full names of the tenants and addresses of their qualifying dwellings;
- address of the property to which it applies; and
- the name and address of the auditor.

It must specify:

- any documents or description of documents which the landlord is required to supply to the auditor;
- any documents which the landlord is required to afford facilities for inspection;
- (under the appropriate sections of the Act); and
- the date upon which the auditor proposes to carry out any inspection of the common parts, which must be not less than one month or more than two months after the date of the notice.

25.8 What happens once the notice is served?

The landlord must within one month of the notice supply the documents requested and afford facilities for the inspection of the specified documents.

The landlord may serve notice objecting to the supply of certain documents but not of any which would be required under section 22 of the LTA 1985 – the notice must contain reasons.

The landlord may object to the date of the inspection of the common parts but must propose another falling within the two month deadline.

If the notice is not complied with within two months of the notice, an application for an order compelling compliance may be made. The application must be made within four months of the notice date.

25.9 What happens if there is a superior landlord?

If there is a superior landlord section 82 of the *Leasehold Reform Housing and Urban Development Act* 1993 applies:

82.

(1) Where the landlord is required by a notice under section 80 to supply any summary falling within section 79(2)(a), and any information necessary for complying with the notice so far as relating to any such summary is in the possession of a superior landlord—

(a)   the landlord shall make a written request for the relevant information to the person who is his landlord (and so on, if that person is himself not the superior landlord);

(b)   the superior landlord shall comply with that request within the period of one month beginning with the date of the making of the request; and

(c)   the landlord who received the notice shall then comply with it so far as relating to any such summary within the time allowed by section 81(1) or such further time, if any, as is reasonable.

(2) Where—

(a)   the landlord is required by a notice under section 80 to afford the auditor facilities for inspection or taking copies or extracts in respect of any documents or description of documents specified in the notice, and

(b)   any of the documents in question is in the custody or under the control of a superior landlord,

the landlord shall on receiving the notice inform the auditor as soon as may be of that fact and of the name and address of the superior landlord, and the auditor may then give the superior landlord a notice requiring him to afford the facilities in question in respect of the document.

(3) Subsections (3) to (5) and (7) of section 81 shall, with any necessary modifications, have effect in relation to a notice given to a superior landlord under subsection (2) above as they have effect in relation to any such notice given to a relevant person as is mentioned in subsection (3) of that section.

25.10 What happens if the landlord disposes of his or her interest while the notice is current?

If the landlord disposes of his or her interest while the notice is current section 83 of the LRHUD *Leasehold Reform Housing and Urban Development Act* 1993 applies:

83.

(1) Where—

(a) a notice has been given to a landlord under section 80, and

(b) at a time when any obligations arising out of the notice remain to be discharged by him—

(i) he disposes of the whole or part of his interest as landlord of the qualifying tenants of the constituent dwellings, and

(ii) the person acquiring any such interest of the landlord is in a position to discharge any of those obligations to any extent,

that person shall be responsible for discharging those obligations to that extent, as if he had been given the notice under that section.

(2) If the landlord is, despite any such disposal, still in a position to discharge those obligations to the extent referred to in subsection (1), he shall remain responsible for so discharging them; but otherwise the person referred to in that subsection shall be responsible for so discharging them to the exclusion of the landlord.

(3) Where a person is so responsible for discharging any such obligations (whether with the landlord or otherwise)—

(a) references to the landlord in section 81 shall be read as including, or as, references to that person to such extent as is appropriate to reflect his responsibility for discharging those obligations; but

(b) in connection with the discharge of any such obligations by that person, that section shall apply as if any reference to the date of the giving of the notice under section 80 were a reference to the date of the disposal referred to in subsection (1).

(4) Where—

(a)　a notice has been given to a relevant person under section 79, and

(b)　at a time when any obligations arising out of the notice remain to be discharged by him, he ceases to be a relevant person, but

(c)　he is, despite ceasing to be a relevant person, still in a position to discharge those obligations to any extent,

he shall nevertheless remain responsible for discharging those obligations to that extent; and section 81 shall accordingly continue to apply to him as if he were still a relevant person.

(5) Where—

(a)　a notice has been given to a landlord under section 80, or

(b)　a notice has been given to a relevant person under section 79,

then during the period of twelve months beginning with the date of that notice, no subsequent such notice may be given to the landlord or (as the case may be) that person on behalf of any persons who, in relation to the earlier notice, were qualifying tenants of the constituent dwellings.

26

Calculations for Rent Act or fair rent registrations

The calculation of allowable service charges for fair rent applications is a skill in itself but it is worthwhile taking a little time to familiarise yourself with the rules to ensure that a correct claim is made. This chapter will consider:

- Variable and fixed service charges
- What services may be claimed?
- What may not be claimed?
- The treatment of capital expenditure
- Administration supervision and profit on services
- Apportionments
- Rates, water and council tax charges on the dwelling
- The calculation and claim
- Example service charge and depreciation calculation
- Frequently asked questions

26.1 Variable and fixed service charges

Certain tenancy agreements contain provisions to allow for variable service charges following on from which the registered rent contains provision for the service element to be variable. The scope of this book does not extend to discussing the specifics of these cases and care should be taken to ensure that you are aware of the rules covering them.

The more common situation is that there is no specific provision in the agreement for a variable service charge and for the Landlord's repairing obligations to be covered by section 11 of the LTA 1985. Following on from this the landlord cannot claim for costs for which he or she is responsible but services which are not covered by this section can be claimed for and they are often wide-ranging.

The one general exception to this involves water charges, particularly where communal metering has been adopted since the tenancy began and the tenant is responsible within his or her agreement for paying the water rates. In these cases the rent officer should be asked to register the rent subject to water and sewerage charges being payable in addition to the registered rent.

26.2 What services may be claimed?

The list of items which may be treated as services has increased as new facilities (such as satellite systems) have become available but basically they include:

- **porters and on-site staff** – including their salaries, pensions, expenses, all costs involved with on-site accommodation (e.g. costs of maintaining repairing and renting it and a rent or notional rent upon it). Council tax and utility bills and any other reasonable expenses may also be included. In a similar vein, if on-site offices or other facilities are provided these can also be included;
- **lifts** – the costs of running and servicing lifts including repairs, emergency telephones, power supplies, statutory inspections and insurance all come within the services calculation;
- **heating and hot water** – fuel, maintenance of plant including communal hot water tanks and communal radiators and pipes as well as insurance of them are all covered together with the costs of energy consultants. It must however be noted that the costs of repair of any installations within the dwelling other than communal pipes passing through it are not covered;
- **ventilation and air conditioning** – fuel, servicing, insurance and other costs should be included;
- **common parts** – basically services to the common parts are covered and include cleaners, cleaning materials, light bulbs, heating and lighting, window cleaning, provision of refuse sacks or storage containers and removal of refuse. Emergency lighting and fire alarms as well as fire fighting or prevention equipment and many health and safety requirements are all classed as services;

- **communal systems** – aerials and satellite provision together with door entry systems and other modern communal systems (e.g. cable services) can all be included;
- **other contracts** – to an extent the list is very wide-ranging and the service charge costs incurred need to be analysed to decide what can be included – pest control contracts and warden call systems are just two examples;
- **gardens and grounds** – here again all reasonable costs may be included (gardeners, plants, lighting, etc. are obvious examples but any other expenditure should also be considered);
- **car parks** – the cost of marking out and signage of communal car parks may be included;
- **communal facilities** – the costs of maintaining communal facilities including fuel, maintenance, rental of equipment, etc. are allowable. These facilities range from halls to laundry rooms and kitchens, but nowadays the range increasingly includes sports and keep fit provision. Insurance in connection with provision of the service is also allowable; and
- **furniture, carpets and common parts installations** – repairs and maintenance of furniture, furnishings, etc. provided in the common parts may be included in the calculation and you should not forget items like chandeliers, pictures, mirrors and other particularly expensive items often featured in entrance halls.

26.3 What may not be claimed?

Repair, maintenance and insurance of the dwelling structure (including the building within which the dwelling is situated) and fixtures, fittings and the installations within the dwelling itself specified within section 11 LTA 1985 may not be claimed. This includes:

- **repairing and decorating the communal halls stairways and passages** – this differentiates the structural repair and basic decoration of these areas from those items, previously mentioned which are allowable;
- **provision of fixtures and fittings within the dwelling** – this includes radiators and heating equipment;
- **white goods within a dwelling** – those in communal areas are treated as a service;
- **interior decoration of dwellings;**

- **landlord direct costs** – any amount of staff costs which can be attributed to the direct benefit of the landlord or any other third party rather than general service matters (e.g. If the porter is used to show potential tenants around flats or undertake repairs to the landlord's own flats during his or her working hours, the cost of this cannot be claimed). A certain amount of common sense needs to be used in that a general minor service available to all flats will not come within this definition.

26.4 The treatment of capital expenditure

So far we have dealt with those items which can be claimed based on day to day expenditure. We have not included the costs of capital equipment as the tenant, who theoretically has a short-term tenancy cannot be expected to cover these costs as they are incurred. The rules do however allow for depreciation allowances to be claimed. It is well worth looking at this area as in many cases, especially in mansion blocks, the claim can be substantial.

Basically most items of capital equipment connected with the provision of services can be included in the depreciation schedule – this can include anything from a garden spade to a combined heat and power unit as well as the hall carpet and the garden seat.

The basic method of calculation is to take the capital cost of each item and write it off over a given number of years which should equate to its expected useful life. This presents several problems in that this assessment needs to be carried out and you will require full details of all allowable capital expenditure. If you manage the whole building yourself this should not be a problem but if it is managed by others you may need to make enquiries and exercise the rights under the LTA 1985 as amended to inspect the various bills for the property. It is particularly recommended that section 20 notices regarding major works in this field are kept and used to assist in calculations.

The actual depreciation term will of course vary according to the items involved. The Institute of Rent Officers Education Trust used to publish a very useful volume on services but I understand that this is now long out of print and the Trust and Institute are no longer in existence.

The guide periods in that publication were as follows:

- lift – 25–30 years;
- lift with comprehensive insurance – 50 years;
- central heating boiler – 10–20 years;
- carpets – 10–12 years;
- furniture – 10–12 years;
- laundry equipment – 5–8 years;
- lawn mower – 5–8 years;
- refuse containers – 10 years;
- fire alarms – 10 years;
- fire fighting equipment – 10–12 years;
- door entry phone – 15–20 years;
- warden call system – 10–15 years;
- emergency lighting – 20 years;
- TV aerial – 20 years;
- cooker – 5–8 years; and
- refrigerator – 5–8 years.

The authors would stress (as they did) that these are only guides and that in this day and age some can now be seen as wishful thinking, **but** it must be remembered that additions should be added every time a new calculation is made and that this should include all expenditure on capital parts (e.g. new lift motors, video recording machines for CCTV systems, upgrades to TV aerials, etc.). In all cases the depreciation should be calculated to reflect the reasonable working life of the item and if it differs from the above an explanation of why, accompanying the rent application would not be out of place.

26.5 Administration supervision and profit on services

When all the calculations have been made there is a further allowance to be taken for administration and profit on services. The figures can vary but a charge of ten per cent for administration and five per cent for profit is not out of place. Interestingly this is not allowable against a notional item but is against actual items. It is not allowable against depreciation.

26.6 Apportionments

The best starting point for apportioning service charges must be with the apportionment actually paid by the landlord however, if this is not deemed to be fair, alterations may be made. We cannot possibly deal with every situation in this chapter but the final charge should reflect a fair cost to the tenant of the services he or she receives even if in some circumstances that differs from what the landlord actually has to pay.

26.7 Rates, water and council tax on the dwelling

(Not to be confused with charges relating to service areas dealt with elsewhere.)

This is one of those areas where changes in legislation have led to problems. Things used to be simple in that the fair rent either included them (generally but not always, where they were paid communally) or it did not – this was noted on the registration.

The introduction of communal water metering with resultant savings generally has led to these charges moving from the tenant to the service charge. It may however be possible to have this element of the charge noted as variable and charged in addition to the fair rent. If this can be done, it should be, so as to avoid falling foul of the rent capping rules.

You should then make sure that you remember to recover it!

Council tax on the dwelling itself does not generally form part of the services but if contractually payable by the landlord it should be noted separately on the rent application.

26.8 The calculation and claim

Having gathered together all available information regarding costs and charges relating to the above a service charge claim should be put together. This can be based upon a reasonable estimate of known costs but must only include those costs which are allowable. The final figures may well look very different from the service charge estimate for the building – generally this results in a lower figure but this is not always the case.

26.9 Example service charge and depreciation calculation

Appendix 5 includes an example of a service charge and depreciation calculation which is by no means exhaustive and the actual accounts will vary from building to building. The schedule of additions to the depreciable amounts is necessary to produce the cost column which is then divided by the number of years of allowable depreciation to obtain the total annual depreciation.

The annual depreciation in each case should be:

> Total cost of items divided by number of years over which depreciation is allowed

The total annual depreciation is:

> The sum of all the annual depreciation allowances for the year

For illustrative purposes there is not a column for each year but the pre-1998 column should refer to sums incurred during the depreciation period. In other words it should not include items which have already been fully written off.

When the allowable services have been calculated and management, profit and depreciation added it then only remains to apply the apportionment for the subject flat to this in order to achieve the services claim for that unit.

26.10 Frequently asked questions

Do I need to let the rent officer or the tenant have the service charge accounts and budget for the property?

No – the calculation submitted to the rent officer will be passed on to the tenant but the rent officer or rent assessment committee may make their own calculations based on their own knowledge and experience even if you do supply the actual ones. Proof of the actual costs incurred may help especially if at first sight they appear high.

In a similar vein, if the budget for the property is habitually under stated, it would not be unreasonable to provide calculations based on actual historic costs incurred provided that they were expected to continue.

Can I include a reserve fund?

No – the calculation refers to the actual cost of services not provision for future capital costs.

Why does the rent officer include a sum for fuel charges not counting for rent allowance?

This is part of the service charge but is not eligible for housing benefit. Other benefits are deemed to cover fuel costs and to avoid double payments to claimants this assessment is made. As the rent officer is making calculations this is done at the same time to avoid further work should it be required.

Appendix 1: Residential sector sample service charge accounts

Sample set of residential service charge accounts.

(Note: These may be superseded by a prescribed set should the government bring one in).

Service charge income and expenditure account

	2006	2005
INCOME		
Service charges demanded for period	220,000	190,000
Insurance claims recoveries	0	0
Brought forward surplus (undesirable)	0	0
Interest received	125	120
Transfers from reserve fund		14,443
Other (Specify)	0	0
Total	**220,125**	**204,563**

EXPENDITURE		
Common utilities (includes common parts but also communal systems)		
Gas	30,000	27,500
Electricity	5,555	5,432
Water	10,504	9,650
Oil	0	0
Insurance (specify different policies)	7,550	7,356

Regular expenditure and maintenance (specify e.g.)

Cleaning	4,500	4,300
Gardening	2,200	2,000
Window cleaning	545	545
Door entry	1,200	1,200
CCTV	1,000	1,000
TV aerials	500	500
Displays	350	350
Fire alarm	450	450

Repairs (specify by category)

Internal	2,500	2,500
External	4,250	4,00
Lifts insurance	525	500
Lifts contract	1,010	975
Lift repairs	1,000	1,000
Boilers insurance	250	240
Boilers contract	2,150	2,000
Boilers repairs	2,000	2,000
Contractor costs (e.g. security guards)	7,500	6,790

Staff costs

Salaries, NIC, etc.	42,500	40,000
Agency staff	5,000	5,000

Staff accommodation

Rent	9,800	9,500
Council tax	1,400	1,300
Utilities	800	750
Telephone		
Equipment	500	450

Administration costs

Postage and office supplies	200	200
On site computers and office equipment	300	300

Other administration costs

Legal and professional fees	4,000	4,000
Managing agent fees (You may wish to show fees net and gross of VAT)	22,000	21,000
Other professional fees	5,000	4,750
Accountant's fees	650	625

Other costs (specify)

Qualifying long-term agreements (specify)

Subtotal day-to-day expenditure	**177,689**	**168,063**
Major works expenditure (specify) (it is desirable to have this all here but do not include items specifically charged in the reserve fund account)	25,750	36,500
Subtotal	**203,439**	**204,563**
Transfers to reserve fund	16,686	0
Total expenditure	**220,125**	**204,563**
Balancing charge due	0	0
Credit for year	0	0

RESERVE FUND ACCOUNT

	2006	2005
Balance brought forward from previous year	269,039	275,232
Contributions received	16,686	0
Transfers to service charge fund	0	14,443
Interest received	8,130	8,250
Reserve fund expenditure (specify all unless dealt with in service charge accounts)		
Balance carried forward	**293,855**	**269,039**

SERVICE CHARGE BALANCE SHEET
31st December 2006

	2006	2005
ASSETS		
Year-end balancing charges due from lessees	0	0
Other arrears due from lessees	2,765	3,579
Money in bank account (specify if more than one)	1,650	750
Outstanding insurance claims agreed by insurers	0	0
Other debtors (specify)	0	0
Subtotal assets	**4,415**	**4,329**
LIABILITIES		
Creditors (specify here or by note)	2,250	2,150
Due to reserve fund	0	0
Service charges received in advance	2,165	2,179
Subtotal liabilities	**4,415**	**4,329**
Total	**0**	**0**
Represented by:		
Accumulated funds (undesirable)	0	0
Other credit sums (specify)	0	0
Total	0	0

RESERVE FUND BALANCE SHEET

	2006	2005
ASSETS		
Arrears due from lessees	0	0
Money in bank account (specify if more than one)	293,855	269,039

Due from service charge fund	0	0
Other debtors (specify)	0	0
Subtotal assets	**293,855**	**269,039**

LIABILITIES

Creditors (specify here or by note)	0	0
Due to service charge	0	0
Funds received in advance	0	0
Subtotal liabilities	**0**	**0**

Total	**293,855**	**269,039**
Represented by:		
Accumulated funds	293,855	269,039
Other credit sums (specify)	0	0
Total	**293,855**	**269,039**

Important notes:

In a case where the expenditure is extensive then if the income is placed after the expenditure rather than before it may be easier to read and tie-in for the lessees as the total income and expenditure will come on the same page.

It is also important to deal with balancing charges for a previous year in such a way as not to show them as income due for the current period – the lessees need to know the actual annual cost of running the account in any given year and year-on-year balancing charges can distort this unless they are dealt with so that they do not.

Section 21 of the LTA 1985 as amended by CLRA 2002 provides for a prescribed form of accounts which will take precedence over this example if and when it is enacted.

It is very important that section 21 certificates are issued to conform with the Act. Before issuing accounts you should consider them in the light of the wording of the statute as amended at the time to ensure that they comply.

Appendix 2: Commercial standard account code descriptions

The cost codes are not intended to represent an exhaustive list, but are used for illustrative purposes only.

Owners and managing agents are encouraged to include additional cost codes where this will facilitate greater transparency and clarity with regard to the expenditure incurred or proposed. However, to maintain industry standards and to facilitate benchmark comparison, it is suggested that the cost class and cost category structure is not altered.

Cost Category	
Cost Code	
MANAGEMENT	
1 **Management fees**	
Management fees	Owner or managing agent fees for managing and administering building services excluding rent collection etc.
2 **Accounting fees**	
S/C audit fees	Auditor's fees to review the year-end service charge reconciliation
3 **Site management resources**	
Staff costs	Direct employment or contract costs for provision of staff for management of on-site facilities.
Receptionists/concierge	Direct employment or contract costs for provision of reception and concierge staff, including associated administrative and training costs
Site accommodation (rent/rates)	Rent, service charge and rates associated with site management accommodation
Office costs (telephones/stationery)	Costs of equipping and running site management office

	Petty cash	Miscellaneous minor expenditure incurred in relation to site management duties
	Help desk/call centre/information centre	Operational costs for providing help desk/call centre/information centre facilities
4	**Health, safety and environmental management**	
	Landlord's risk assessments, audits and reviews	Consultancy fees and other costs associated with provision and review of owner's health and safety management systems

UTILITIES

5	**Electricity**	
	Electricity	Electricity supply to common part and retained areas and central plant excluding occupier direct consumption.
	Electricity procurement/consultancy	Consultancy and procurement fees for negotiating electricity supply contract and auditing of energy consumption
	Fuel (standby electrical power)	Fuel oil to run any standby electrical power systems
6	**Gas**	
	Gas	Gas supply to owner's central plant, excluding occupier direct consumption
	Gas procurement/consultancy	Consultancy and procurement fees for negotiating gas supply contract and auditing of energy consumption
7	**Fuel oil (heating)**	
	Fuel oil	Fuel oil supply to owner's central plant, excluding occupier direct consumption
	Fuel oil procurement/consultancy	Consultancy and procurement fees for negotiating oil supply contract and auditing of energy consumption
8	**Water**	
	Water and sewerage charges	Water supply to central plant, common part and retained areas excluding occupier direct consumption
	Water consultancy	Consultancy fees incurred in reviewing water usage

SOFT SERVICES

9	**Security**	
	Security guarding	Direct employment or contract costs incurred in providing building security guarding
	Security systems	Servicing and maintenance of building security systems (e.g. CCTV/access control/intruder alarm)

10 Cleaning and environmental	
Internal cleaning	Cleaning of internal common part and retained areas
External cleaning	Cleaning of external common part and retained areas
Window cleaning	
Hygiene services/toiletries	Cleaning and servicing of common parts toilet accommodation
Carpets/mats hire	Provision of dust and rain mats to common parts
Waste management	Refuse collection and waste management services provided for building occupiers
Pest control	Pest control services provided to common part and retained areas
Internal floral displays	Providing and maintaining floral displays within the common parts
External landscaping	Provision and maintenance of external landscaped areas and special features.
Seasonal decorations	Provision and maintenance of seasonal decorations to common parts.
11 Marketing and promotions	
Events	Promotional events
Marketing	Marketing and advertising in accordance with marketing strategy
Research	Research into local market conditions, customer surveys, etc.
Staff costs	Direct employment or contract costs for provision of marketing and promotional activity
Landlord's contribution to marketing	Financial contributions made by landlord towards marketing and promotions
Local authority contribution to marketing	Financial contributions made by local authority towards marketing and promotions
HARD SERVICES	
12 Mechanical and electrical services	
Mechanical and electrical maintenance contract	Planned maintenance to the owner's mechanical and electrical services, including contractor's health and safety compliance
Mechanical and electrical repairs	Repair works to the owner's mechanical and electrical services

Mechanical and electrical inspections and consultancy	Auditing quality of maintenance works, condition of mechanical and electrical plant and health and safety compliance
Life safety systems maintenance	Planned maintenance works to the owner's fire protection, emergency lighting and other specialist life safety systems, including contractor's health and safety compliance
Life safety systems repairs	Repair works to the owner's fire protection, emergency lighting and other specialist life safety systems
Life safety systems inspections and consultancy	Auditing quality of maintenance works, condition of plant and health and safety compliance
13 Lift and escalators	
Lift maintenance contract	Planned maintenance works to lifts in the common part and retained areas, including contractor's health and safety compliance
Lift repairs	Repair works to common parts lifts
Lift inspections and consultancy	Auditing quality of maintenance works, condition of lift plant and health and safety compliance
Escalator maintenance contract	Planned maintenance works to escalators in the common part and retained areas, including contractor's health and safety compliance
Escalator repairs	Repair works to common parts escalators
Escalator inspections and consultancy	Auditing quality of maintenance works, condition of escalator plant and health and safety compliance
14 Suspended access equipment	
Suspended access maintenance contract	Planned maintenance works to the owner's suspended access equipment, including contractor's health and safety compliance
Suspended access repairs	Repair works to the owner's suspended access equipment
Suspended access inspections and consultancy	Auditing quality of maintenance works, condition of suspended access equipment and health and safety compliance
15 Fabric repairs and maintenance	
Internal repairs and maintenance	Repair and maintenance of internal building fabric, common part and retained areas
External repairs and maintenance	Repair and maintenance of external building fabric, structure, external common part and retained areas
Redecorations	Re-decoration and decorative repairs

INCOME	**Distinct activities that yield a true income to the service charge account**
16 Interest	
Interest	Interest received on service charge monies held within owner's or agent's bank account
17 Income from commercialisation	**Income yielded from any facilities installed and/or maintained at the occupier's expense**
Car park income	
Vending machine income	
Other	
Operational expenses	
Contract charges	Overheads, expenses and operational costs incurred in providing any of the above facilities
Repairs and maintenance	
Staff costs	
INSURANCE	**Landlord's engineering insurances**
18 Engineering insurance	
Engineering insurance	
Engineering inspections	
19 All risks insurance cover	**Landlord's all risk insurance costs**
Buildings insurance	
Loss of rent insurance	
Public and property owner's liability	
Landlord's contents	
20 Terrorism insurance	**Landlord's terrorism insurance costs**
Terrorism	
EXCEPTIONAL EXPENDITURE	
21 Buildings insurance	
Project works	Exceptional and one-off project works, over and above routine operational costs
Refurbishments	
Plant replacement	

Major repairs	
22 Forward funding	
Sinking funds	Forward funding of specific major replacement projects (e.g. plant and equipment replacements, roof replacements)
Reserve funds	Forward funding of specific periodic works to even-out fluctuations in annual service charge costs (e.g. internal/external redecorations)
Depreciation charge	Depreciation charge in lieu of sinking/replacement fund contribution of major plant and equipment

Additional notes

Separate cost categories are **not** to be used for single service activities provided across different elements of a subject property, e.g. estate, car park, etc. Where multiple schedules are not used, it may be necessary to repeat certain cost codes to make a clear distinction between costs, i.e. fabric repairs and maintenance/security/cleaning and environmental costs might include duplicate codes for estate and car park charges.

Suspended access equipment includes all forms of high-level access equipment maintenance, i.e. hatchways, eye-bolt, fall address and cradles.

Appendix 3: Landlord's surveyor's service charge certificate (commercial)

Note that if any residential property is included Section 21 LTA 1985 will apply and you should refer to its requirements as it is a criminal offence for a landlord not to comply.

Landlord's surveyor's service charge certificate

Property:

I hereby certify that, according to the information available to me, the attached statement of the service charge expenditure records the true cost to the Landlord of providing the services to the premises for the period [ ] to [ ] in accordance with the terms of the lease.

Signed: Date:

NAME and
QUALIFICATIONS:

Title:

For and on
behalf of:

As agents for:

Appendix 4: Detailed expenditure report (Commercial)

Detailed expenditure report

Detailed expenditure report for the period [DATE FROM] to [DATE TO]

Property address:

	Expenditure Total	Shedule 1 Estate	Schedule 2 Building 1	Schedule 3 Building 2
	(£)	(£)	(£)	(£)
MANAGEMENT				
1 Management fees				
Management fees	60,000	10,000	25,000	25,000
2 Accounting fees				
S/C audit fees	1,600	1,600		
3 Site management resources				
Staff costs	15,000	15,000		
Receptionist/ concierge	50,000		26,600	23,400
Site accommodation (rent/rates)	4,335	4,335		
Office costs (telephone/ stationary)	1,800	1,800		
4 Health, safety and environmental				
Risk assessments and audits	10,000	10,000		
Subtotal	**142,735**	**42,735**	**51,600**	**48,400**
UTILITIES				
5 Electricity				
Electricity	224,000		112,000	112,000
Electricity procurement/ consultancy	5,600	5,600		

258

Fuel (standby electrical power)	300	300		
6 Gas				
Gas	10,000		5,000	5,000
Gas procurement/ consultancy	1,050	1,050		
7 Fuel oil (heating)				
8 Water				
Water and sewerage charges	7,000		3,500	3,500
Subtotal	**247,950**	**6,950**	**120,500**	**120,500**

SOFT SERVICES

9 Security

Security guarding	132,000	132,000		
Security systems	12,100	5,500	3,500	3,100
10 Cleaning and environmental				
Internal cleaning	91,200		38,400	52,800
External cleaning	15,500	15,500		
Window cleaning	22,800		9,600	13,200
Hygiene services/ toiletries	8,180		4,500	3,680
Waste management	9,050	9,050		
Pest control	1,600	700	500	400
Seasonal decorations	1,000		500	500
Internal floral displays	9,400		4,800	4,600
Estate cleaning	18,000	18,000		
External landscaping	9,000	9,000		
11 Marketing and promotions				
Subtotal	**329,830**	**189,750**	**61,800**	**78,280**

259

HARD SERVICES

12 Mechanical and electrical services

Mechanical and electrical maintenance contract	151,250	20,000	63,000	68,250
Mechanical and electrical repairs	16,250	2,150	6,750	7,350
Mechanical and electrical inspections and consultancy	7,500	7,500		
Life safety systems maintenance	11,350	2,350	5,000	4,000
Life safety systems repairs	1,620	750		870

13 Lift and escalators

Lift maintenance contracts	21,000		12,000	9,000
Lift repairs	3,500		2,000	1,500

14 Suspended access equipment

Maintenance contract	5,100		2,700	2,400
Repairs	200		100	100
Inspections and consultancy				

15 Fabric repairs and maintenance

Internal repairs and maintenance	50,000		35,000	15,000
External repairs and maintenance	6.775			6,775
Redecorations	5,700		5,700	
Estate repairs and maintenance	32,100	32,100		
Car park repairs and maintenance	4,750	4,750		
Subtotal	**317,095**	**69,600**	**132,250**	**115,245**

INCOME

16 Interest

Interest	-1,068	-332	-373	-368

17 Income from commercialisation

Subtotal	**-1,068**	**-332**	**-373**	**-368**

INSURANCE

18 Engineering insurance

Engineering insurance	900		500	400

19 All risks insurance cover

20 Terrorism insurance

Subtotal	**900**		**500**	**400**

EXCEPTIONAL EXPENDITURE

21 Major works

Plant replacement	92,483		92,483	

22 Forward funding

Sinking funds	-92,483		-92,483	
Subtotal	**0**		**0**	

GRAND TOTAL	**1,037,442**	**308,703**	**366,277**	**362,462**

Appendix 5: Service charge calculation for a 'fair rent' application

UTOPIA LUXURY MANSIONS 2004-2005 SERVICES	(£)
ITEM OF EXPENDITURE	
STAFF	
WAGES OVERTIME NI PENSIONS	200,000.00
RELIEF PORTER and SECURITY	72,000.00
Sundries including Uniforms	9,000.00
STAFF EXPENSES	
COUNCIL TAX and WATER RATES	2,120.00
TELEPHONE and RADIO	3,753.00
REPAIRS to staff accommodation	1,110.00
RENT ON PORTERS FLATS	48,163.00
ELECTRICITY – GAS STAFF ACCOMMODATION	750.00
POWER SUPPLIES	
ELECTRICITY	25,000.00
GAS	65,928.00
GENERAL MAINTENANCE	
BOILERS and AIR CONDITIONING REPAIRS	12,500.00
DOOR ENTRY SYSTEM	7,065.00
SECURITY (CCTV)	2,120.00
FIRE PROTECTION	7,434.00
CLEANING	41,969.00
ALLOWABLE REPAIRS AND RENEWALS	5,000.00
TV and SATELLITE AERIAL	14,498.00
PEST CONTROL	10,117.00

SUPPLIES	
CLEANING MATERIALS and	5,250.00
LIGHT BULBS and SUNDRIES	3,000.00
LIFTS	
CONTRACT and REPAIRS	15,300.00
INSURANCES	
ENGINEERING and LIFT	1,500.00
EMPLOYERS PROTECTION	125.00
HEALTH and SAFETY	1,500.00
Subtotal	**555,202.00**
MANAGEMENT 10 per cent	55,520.20
LANDLORDS PROFIT 5 per cent	27,760.10
Subtotal	**638,482.30**
DEPRECIATION SEE SCHEDULE	80,646.15
TOTAL	**719,128.45**

SERVICE CHARGE APPORTIONMENTS		
	per cent	**(£)**
Flat no.	Apportionment	Due
5	0.436	3,135.40
65	0.529	3,804.19
25	0.626	4,501.74
49	0.685	4,926.03

DEPRECIATION SCHEDULE		COST*	ANNUAL DEPRECIATION
BOILER, TANKS ETC	15YEARS	622,053	41,470.20
LIFTS	25YEARS	246,788	9,871.52.00
CARPETS	10 YEARS	72,456	7,245.60
FIRE EXTINGUISHERS	10 YEARS	4,960	496.00
FURNITURE	10 YEARS	16,756	1,675.60
TV AERIAL and ENTRY PHONE	20YEARS	66,781	3,339.05
GARDEN STATUES	25YEARS	16,752	670.08
CHANDELIERS	12YEARS	13,256	1,104.67
CCTV	10YEARS	21,915	2,191.50
AIR CONDITIONING	15 YEARS	188,729	12,581.93
TOTAL			**80,646.15**

*See table opposite for detail of cost

ADDITIONS TO DEPRECIABLE AMOUNTS	year-ending									
	PRE 1998 **	1998	1999	2000	2001	2002	2003	2004	2005	TOTAL
BOILER, TANKS ETC	70,982	25,500	24,519	22,540	73,256	13,256	47,000	345,000		622,053
LIFTS	52,000					119,850	74,938			246,788
CARPETS	72,456									72,456
FIRE EXTINGUISHERS	2,560							2,400		4,960
FURNITURE	14,556							2,200		16,756
TV AERIAL and ENTRY PHONE	12,489						35,290	19,002		66,781
GARDEN STATUES	16,752									16,752
CHANDELIERS	13,256									13,256
CCTV	14,290			3,000		2,500		2,125		21,915
AIR CONDITIONING			44,844	54,635	89,250					188,729

** Items are only included within depreciation period

Index